THE DIALOGUE
OF SOLOMON AND MARCOLF

MIDDLE ENGLISH TEXTS SERIES

The Middle English Texts Series is designed for classroom use. Its goal is to make available to teachers, scholars, and students texts that occupy an important place in the literary and cultural canon but have not been readily available in student editions. The series does not include those authors, such as Chaucer, Langland, or Malory, whose English works are normally in print in good student editions. The focus is, instead, upon Middle English literature adjacent to those authors that teachers need in compiling the syllabuses they wish to teach. The editions maintain the linguistic integrity of the original work but within the parameters of modern reading conventions. The texts are printed in the modern alphabet and follow the practices of modern capitalization, word formation, and punctuation. Manuscript abbreviations are silently expanded, and *u/v* and *j/i* spellings are regularized according to modern orthography. Yogh (ȝ) is transcribed as *g*, *gh*, *y*, or *s*, according to the sound in Modern English spelling to which it corresponds; thorn (þ) and eth (ð) are transcribed as *th*. Distinction between the second person pronoun and the definite article is made by spelling the one *thee* and the other *the*, and final *-e* that receives full syllabic value is accented (e.g., *charité*). Hard words, difficult phrases, and unusual idioms are glossed either in the right margin or at the foot of the page. Explanatory and textual notes appear at the end of the text, often along with a glossary. The editions include short introductions on the history of the work, its merits and points of topical interest, and brief working bibliographies.

This series is published in association with the University of Rochester.

Medieval Institute Publications is a program of
The Medieval Institute, College of Arts and Sciences

 WESTERN MICHIGAN UNIVERSITY

THE DIALOGUE OF SOLOMON AND MARCOLF: A DUAL-LANGUAGE EDITION FROM LATIN AND MIDDLE ENGLISH PRINTED EDITIONS

Edited by
Nancy Mason Bradbury and Scott Bradbury

TEAMS • Middle English Texts Series

MEDIEVAL INSTITUTE PUBLICATIONS
Western Michigan University
Kalamazoo

Library of Congress Cataloging-in-Publication Data

The dialogue of Solomon and Marcolf : a dual-language edition from Latin and Middle
English printed editions / edited by Nancy Mason Bradbury and Scott Bradbury.
    p. cm.
  "Published for TEAMS (The Consortium for the Teaching of the Middle Ages) in
Association with the University of Rochester."
  Includes bibliographical references.
  ISBN 978-1-58044-180-3 (pbk. : alk. paper)
  1. Salomon et Marcolphus. 2. Dialogues, Latin (Medieval and modern)–Translations into
English. 3. Dialogues, Latin (Medieval and modern)–History and criticism. 4. Solomon,
King of Israel–In literature. I. Bradbury, Nancy M. II. Bradbury, Scott. III. Salomon et
Marcolphus. English & Latin.
  PA8420.S14D53 2013
  872'.03–dc23
                                                                                    2012033896

ISBN 978-1-58044-180-3

P   5   4   3   2   1

❧ CONTENTS

LIST OF ILLUSTRATIONS

ACKNOWLEDGMENTS

We are grateful to Smith College for funding our travel to Oxford and Cambridge to examine the printed editions of our texts housed in their university libraries. We thank our colleagues Eglal Doss-Quinby and Luc Gilleman for sharing their expertise and Jan M. Ziolkowski for providing us with a prepublication copy of *Solomon and Marcolf*, his comprehensive 2008 study of the Latin work. The editors of *Speculum* graciously gave permission for us to draw in our introduction upon the 2008 article "Rival Wisdom in the Latin *Dialogue of Solomon and Marcolf*" by one of this volume's editors. We salute with gratitude and affection our two meticulous research assistants, Sarah Allen and Teresa Pandolfo. For expert editorial guidance, patience, and good nature, many thanks to John H. Chandler, Martha M. Johnson-Olin, Kara L. McShane, and Russell A. Peck at the University of Rochester and Patricia Hollahan at Medieval Institute Publications. We thank also the National Endowment for the Humanities for its support of the TEAMS Middle English Texts Series.

 **INTRODUCTION**

1. NATURE OF THE PROJECT

The facing texts, Latin and Middle English, presented in this volume preserve a lively, entertaining, and revealing dialogue between the Old Testament wisdom figure, Solomon, and a medieval peasant, Marcolf, ragged and foul-mouthed but quick-witted and verbally adept. The work's traditional Latin title is *Dialogus Salomonis et Marcolfi* (*The Dialogue of Solomon and Marcolf*); from about 1410 to 1550, versions of this dialogue were literary best-sellers by the standards of the day. Their widespread appeal is attested by the survival of Latin versions in some twenty-seven manuscripts and forty-nine early printed editions, as well as translations into a wide variety of late medieval vernaculars, including German, Dutch, Swedish, Italian, English, and Welsh. In 1914, Walter Benary published a critical edition of the Latin dialogue under the title *Salomon et Marcolfus*, using as his base text the manuscript Würzburg, Universitätsbibliothek M.ch.f. 65, which bears the date 1434 on fol. 174r (see below, section 6.b). Benary's Latin text was reprinted by Jan M. Ziolkowski in 2008 under the title *Solomon and Marcolf* with a modern English translation and extensive commentary, a publication that will greatly advance the study of this intriguing work.

The two texts of the *Dialogue* presented here both derive from early printed editions, a Latin version printed c. 1488 and a Middle English translation printed in 1492, both produced in the Antwerp workshop of Gerard (or Gheraert) Leeu.[1] Leeu has been described by historians of printing as "the most original publisher in the Low Countries in the fifteenth century,"[2] and he deserves to be better known to readers of English, for his career overlapped with that of England's first printer, William Caxton. Indeed it is likely that they died in the same year, 1492, shortly after Leeu printed the Middle English text presented in this volume.[3] Leeu began printing books for the English market in the 1480s, little more than a decade after Caxton printed the first book in English. Thus Leeu's edition of *The Dialogue of Solomon and Marcolf* numbers among the very first printed books in English to be issued from outside the Caxton workshops. Leeu's Middle English edition survives in a

---

[1] For the dates, see W. Hellinga and L. Hellinga, *Fifteenth-Century Printing Types*, 1:420.

[2] W. Hellinga and L. Hellinga, *Fifteenth-Century Printing Types*, 1:72.

[3] For more about the career of Leeu, see section 6.c below. The dates of both deaths have been debated, but for Caxton, the evidence points to the first three months of 1492; see Blake, "William Caxton," p. 44. Leeu's death date is sometimes given as 1493 because his last book, an edition of the *Chronicles of England,* did not appear until that year, but W. Hellinga and L. Hellinga, *Fifteenth-Century Printing Types*, 1:73, cite a burial record that places the death between December 3 and 24 of 1492. The colophon to the *Chronicles* (quoted in section 6.c below) testifies that Leeu was already dead when the book appeared in 1493.

single printed edition, now shelved in the Bodleian Library, Oxford, as Tanner 178 (3). Facsimiles are available in the editions by E. Gordon Duff and Donald Beecher and at Early English Books Online.[4]

Our dual-language edition pairs Leeu's Middle English text with the Latin text of the *Dialogue* he printed some four years earlier. Although Leeu's Latin text is the source most likely to have been used by the English translator, no distinctive shared readings decisively link the two and there are a few minor discrepancies between them. Nothing is known about the circumstances under which the English translation was made, but it shares a few readings with a later Dutch translation that are not present in Leeu's Latin text. It is most likely that the earlier Middle English text influenced the later Dutch, but it is not impossible, as one scholar has argued, that a now-lost earlier edition of the surviving Dutch translation influenced or served as the model for the English (see section 6.c below). Whatever its relation to other versions, the Middle English translation that Leeu printed in 1492 corresponds very closely to the text of his Latin print of c. 1488, and thus a reader of our edition with some knowledge of Latin can now compare the English to the extant text most likely to have served as its model. Our explanatory notes emphasize the English text but include comments on the Latin as well, particularly on problems of translation. The Middle English is thoroughly glossed on the text pages. For the general interpretation of the dialogue offered in this introduction as well as the early history of the Latin text, we have drawn upon an article by one of the present editors, Nancy Mason Bradbury, "Rival Wisdom in the Latin *Dialogue of Solomon and Marcolf*," and we thank the journal editors for permission to do so.

To find one's way through the maze of Solomon and Marcolf texts, it is important to recognize that the *Dialogue* survives in various Latin versions, and these versions can differ significantly. For example, the longest of the dialogue's verbal contests is a competitive exchange of proverbs. The fullest manuscripts of the *Dialogue* contain some 138 exchanges (depending on where one begins and stops counting), whereas some manuscripts and all printed editions contain only 88–90 exchanges. When and why this abridgement or bowdler-ization might have occurred will be explored below in section 6.c, but we note that the omitted exchanges are often striking and their absence changes the complexion of the work. Many include scatological retorts from Marcolf, and some others are blasphemous, obscene, or rabidly misogynist. In an appendix, we include the forty-nine exchanges omitted from the proverb contest by the printed versions, supplying the missing exchanges from the standard manuscript-based text edited by Walter Benary, along with our own translations. Our appendix shows how much of its satiric bite the proverb contest loses by this abridgement.

2. IMPORTANCE OF *THE DIALOGUE OF SOLOMON AND MARCOLF*

The Dialogue of Solomon and Marcolf is very much a medieval work; mentions of earlier avatars begin around the year 1000 and are widespread by the thirteenth century.[5] It pits a static clerical authority, represented by Solomon, against an outrageously provocative

---

[4] Duff, ed., *Dialogue or Communing*; Beecher, ed., *Dialogue of Solomon and Marcolphus*; Early English Books Online is available at <http://eebo.chadwyck.com>.

[5] For a full list of the early allusions with original texts and translations, see Ziolkowski, *Solomon and Marcolf*, pp. 316–60.

voice for improvisation and innovation, polarizing these two voices but also bringing them into dialogue. Thus part of its importance for medievalists is as yet another piece of evidence that the intellectual rebirth for which early modern thinkers gave themselves full credit had deep roots in medieval culture. Despite the considerable attention earlier forms of the work attracted, no manuscripts survive prior to 1410, and the earliest print is dated c. 1473. In the cultural climate of the fifteenth and early sixteenth centuries, the explosive collision between Solomon's authoritative wisdom and Marcolf's morally ambiguous cleverness generated enough energy to propel the *Dialogue* into multiple Latin manuscript versions and then into numerous printed editions in Latin and a variety of European vernaculars.

The Latin *Dialogue* and its vernacular translations are better known to scholars of Continental Europe than they are to Anglo-American medievalists. Versions of the work were especially popular in German-speaking lands from the fifteenth to the seventeenth centuries, first in Latin and then in the vernacular, and German scholars have long taken an active interest in it.[6] In Italy, this dialogue inspired a minor classic still widely available in paperback, Giulio Cesare Croce's *Bertoldo* (1606), and thus a modern Italian scholar, Maria Corti, calls the Latin dialogue "a well-known text, familiar within our culture."[7] Scholars of Old French and Anglo-French know Marcolf from his mordant contributions to a series of rhymed proverb exchanges.[8] Interest in the dialogue on the part of Middle English scholars stems in part from new attention to a "Marcolf" poem by John Audelay.[9]

The Dialogue of Solomon and Marcolf has also played a significant role in the history of medieval scholarship via its influence on Mikhail Bakhtin's *Rabelais and His World*. Readers are often struck by how "Bakhtinian" or "carnivalesque" Marcolf's provocative contributions seem, but it would be more accurate to call Bakhtin's theory of popular culture "Marcolfian." The *Dialogue* was one of a relatively small number of medieval (as opposed to ancient, late antique, and early modern) works Bakhtin cited in illustration of his ideas about the subversive and life-affirming potential of "the material bodily lower stratum."[10] Bakhtin uses this phrase to designate the parts of the human body most effaced or even demonized by clerical writings but celebrated in a variety of comic and anti-institutional forms, including jests, drinking songs, and parodies of sacred texts. Like the Latin texts of the *Dialogue*, much of this antiauthoritarian material very likely originated among medieval clerics themselves, as they were the authors and readers, and therefore the most likely parodists, of Medieval Latin literature. Despite its probable origins among medieval clerics (a category that included priests, scholars, monastics, and others educated in Latin), this variegated mass of anti-authoritarian (or anti-institutional) materials incorporated preexisting verbal forms that circulated throughout medieval vernacular culture: forms such as jests, riddles, and popular proverbs. Thus works such as *The Dialogue of Solomon and Marcolf* reveal a resistant spirit that Bakhtin called "the people's festive laughter" to distinguish it from the solemn, penitential

---

[6] Curschmann, "Marcolfus deutsch"; Griese, *Salomon und Markolf*.

[7] Corti, "Models and Antimodels in Medieval Culture," p. 357. For the Latin dialogue as the source of *Bertoldo*, see Cortese-Pagani, "Il 'Bertoldo' de Guilio Cesare Croce ed i suoi fonti."

[8] Hunt, "Solomon and Marcolf."

[9] See Audelay, *Poems and Carols*, ed. Fein; Green, "Marcolf the Fool and Blind John Audelay" and "Langland and Audelay"; Simpson, "Saving Satire after Arundel's *Constitutions*"; and Pearsall, "Audelay's *Marcolf and Solomon* and the Langlandian Tradition."

[10] Bakhtin, *Rabelais*, pp. 368–436.

tone that permeates the official products of medieval institutions.[11] In comparison to the vast amount of devout and institutionally sanctioned literature that survives from the Middle Ages, these mocking and transgressive forms are much rarer, but they nevertheless have an important role to play in helping us to understand the full range of medieval culture.

3. SOLOMON

Although his peasant interlocutor hails from medieval Europe, the Solomon figure of our work draws heavily upon the language and life history of the Old Testament patriarch. The genealogy Solomon recites early in the *Dialogue* derives from scripture, as do many of his speeches. In the Latin texts, Solomon speaks in the accessible, international Latin of the Vulgate Bible. Thus his language contrasts tellingly with Marcolf's more concrete, colloquial, and earthy speech, with its insistent references to the barnyard and to the human body and its animal functions. Vernacular translators such as our unknown English writer easily render the familiar language of Solomon's side of the dialogue while Marcolf's often-cryptic utterances give them much more trouble, as our explanatory notes indicate.

The basic elements that make up Solomon's life and character in this dialogue are already present in the Old Testament account in 3 Kings 3–11: most notably, his possession of extraordinary wisdom, his skill in rendering just judgments, and the threat to his pre-eminence posed by challengers determined to test that fabled wisdom.[12] In a dream the young Solomon asks God for "an understanding heart, to judge thy people, and discern between good and evil" (3 Kings 3:9). Pleased with his request, God grants him "wisdom and understanding exceeding . . . the sand that is on the sea shore" so that he becomes "wiser than all men" (3 Kings 4:29–31). From the beginning, then, Solomon's is a moral wisdom, a faculty that allows him to make just judgments and to hold three thousand proverbs (3 Kings 4:32, Latin Vulgate *parabolae*) in his capacious memory. That Solomon's words derive mainly from the Old Testament wisdom books would make sense to medieval readers, who attributed a substantial part of the wisdom literature of the Old Testament to Solomon, including Proverbs, Ecclesiastes, the Song of Songs, Wisdom, and Ecclesiasticus. The Solomon of the dialogue alludes in the proverb contest (4.5a) to his famous biblical judgment between two women who claim the same child (3 Kings 3:16–28), and the circumstances of the judgment are narrated in more detail in 16.1–4. Even this quintessential example of Solomon's wisdom is undermined in *The Dialogue of Solomon and Marcolf*, however, when Marcolf deliberately recounts a distorted version in order to discredit the king with his female subjects (18.3).

Long before the appearance of the medieval peasant Marcolf, Solomon's reputation for preeminent wisdom had attracted challengers. In the Bible, the queen of Sheba comes "to try him with hard questions" (3 Kings 10:1). According to early Jewish tradition, another biblical figure, Hiram, king of Tyre, competed against Solomon in a riddling contest, as does Marcolf in our dialogue, and Jewish legend also tells of the efforts of the demon

---

[11] Bakhtin, *Rabelais*, pp. 4–15 and 59–123, quotation at p. 12.

[12] Biblical citations in Latin in this volume are from the Vulgate; English translations are from the Douay-Rheims Bible.

Asmodeus to get the better of Solomon.[13] Around the sixth century, the title *Contradictio Salomonis* (or *Interdictio*, depending on the manuscript) appears in a list of books prohibited by a decree falsely attributed to Pope Gelasius (432–96) — this otherwise unknown but apparently controversial work may have recorded another irreverent challenge to Solomon's wisdom. An Anglo-Saxon poem dated to c. 900 represents Solomon debating Saturn, the latter depicted as a Chaldean pagan. This poetic dialogue, known as *Solomon and Saturn II*, makes a single reference to a land of Marcolf — "Marculfes eard" (line 180b).[14] At least another century elapses before the first direct reference to a verbal challenger named Marcolf appears; see our account of Marcolf in the following section and our summary of the *Dialogue*'s prehistory in section 6.a below.[15]

4. MARCOLF

No one has solved the riddle of what connection, if any, exists between the peasant hero of our dialogue and the reference to "Marculfes eard" (Marcolf's land) in the Anglo-Saxon poetic dialogue *Solomon and Saturn II*. If Marcolfus (Marcolphus, Marculfus) is a Latinized version of the Anglo-Saxon or Germanic name Marculf or Marcolf, the name probably derives from *mark-wulf*, 'wolf of the marches or borderlands,'[16] so that even in his name, Marcolf is an unsettling, marginal figure associated with a literal or figurative periphery. In most versions of the *Dialogue*, Marcolf comes to the court of King Solomon in Jerusalem "from the east" (Latin "a parte oriente," Middle English "out of th'este"). Ziolkowski notes that in *Solomon and Saturn II*, Solomon's antagonist Saturn is traveling in eastern lands, where he encounters the mysterious "land of Marculf."[17] The Anglo-Saxon poem thus may help to support the work of early scholars who sought to connect Marcolf with various eastern figures from medieval legend, some of them demonic, who presented early challenges to Solomon.

The earliest reference to Marcolf as a challenger to Solomon's wisdom occurs in the work of Notker Labeo (Notker of St. Gall, 952–1022). Notker objects to various types of profane literature, including works in which Marcolf contends with the proverbs of Solomon, in beautiful words that lack truth.[18] If Notker has in mind a tradition or a work that resembles the extant dialogue, his criticism may acknowledge the verbal agility of some of Marcolf's replies, but reject their irreverence. The large temporal gap that separates passing allusions such as this one from the written texts that emerge in the fifteenth century suggests that earlier versions circulated orally as well as in writing. The wide variation among the surviving texts may also point toward some form of oral transmission. Sabine Griese cites

---

[13] For Hiram, see Ginzberg, *Legends of the Jews*, 4:141–42; for Asmodeus, see Bose, "From Exegesis to Appropriation," pp. 192–93.

[14] Menner, ed., *Poetical Dialogues of Solomon and Saturn*r; see also O'Brien O'Keeffe, "Geographic List of *Solomon and Saturn II*."

[15] For information about confrontations between Solomon and his challengers prior to Marcolf, see Bose, "From Exegesis to Appropriation"; Ziolkowski, *Solomon and Marcolf*, pp. 19–22; and the extensive references cited, especially by the latter.

[16] Menner, ed., *Poetical Dialogues of Solomon and Saturn*, ed. Menner, p. 119.

[17] Ziolkowski, *Solomon and Marcolf*, p. 22.

[18] For text and commentary, see Ziolkowski, *Solomon and Marcolf*, pp. 317–20.

a possible piece of evidence for the oral performance of an earlier version of the dialogue: Lambert of Ardres describes an entertainment at the court of Arnold of Guînes in 1194 that included tales of a variety of figures, including a "Merchulfo" that Griese identifies with Marcolf.[19]

Although there is no direct evidence for such an activity, the dialogue may have been influenced by some sort of irreverent game in which participants in the "Marcolf" role made up scandalous mock-Solomonic proverbs. Certainly the surviving exchanges vary widely in their wit and their crudity. As a bit of much later evidence for such an activity, Natalie Zemon Davis observes that the brief exchange between Solomon and Marcolf mentioned in chapter 33 of François Rabelais' *Gargantua* (1534) sounds very much like a game of "the dozens," an insult-swapping match, as do many of the exchanges in the *Dialogue* itself.[20] In an exchange not present in the versions of the *Dialogue* that survive to us, Rabelais' ambitious courtier Spadassin cites a version of a well-known proverb: "'The man who ventures nothing wins neither horse nor mule,' as Solomon said." To this a seasoned old campaigner replies, "'The man who ventures too much loses both horse and mule,' as Malcon answered."[21] Rabelais' "Malcon" replies with the same sardonic pragmatism we associate with Marcolf, once again set against Solomon's optimistic idealism.

In addition to its possible oral ancestry, the clandestine nature of the Marcolfian tradition, with its scatology, blasphemy, and occasional obscenity could also help to account for the dearth or disappearance of whatever early manuscripts may once have existed. The fullest Latin manuscripts preserve the tradition's razor-sharp edges, with the transgressive verbal parallels Marcolf draws between, for example, wisdom and shit, the evangelists and the supports of a latrine, or the Lord and the anus (Appendix, nos. B 38ab, B 89ab, and B 138ab), but even among the existing manuscripts, omissions and substitutions suggest that softened versions were often more acceptable to transmitters and readers, and by the time of the Latin prints and vernacular translations, the text had been very much sanitized.

Many traces remain of Marcolf's reputation in medieval England. As Malcolm Jones and Michael Camille have shown, Marcolf's antiauthoritarian posture can take quite literal form in the margins of medieval manuscripts, where he bares his posterior to the viewer, as he does to a startled Solomon in the *Dialogue* (24.8–12).[22] Images of Marcolf appeared in a thirteenth-century register of writs, a now-vanished mid-thirteenth-century wall painting (Henry III's "Marcolf" chamber in the palace at Westminster), and two early fourteenth-century psalters. The Marcolf of our dialogue is a skilled wielder of proverbs, and thus it is fitting that a reference to him occurs in the *Proverbs of Hending*, a versified collection of English sayings that circulated in the thirteenth and fourteenth centuries. In the version found in British Library MS Harley 2253, Hending is identified as "Marcolves sone," and at the end of the moral proverbs assigned to Hending in Cambridge University Library MS

---

[19] Griese, *Salomon und Markolf,* pp. 1–2. Lambert of Ardres, *Historia Comitum Ghisnensium,* ed. Heller, p. 607. In English, Lambert of Ardres, *History of the Counts of Guines,* pp. 129–30.

[20] Davis, "Proverbial Wisdom," p. 227.

[21] "Qui ne se adventure, n'a cheval ny mule, ce dist Salomon. Qui trop (dist Echephron) se adventure perd cheval et mulle, respondit Malcon" (*Gargantua,* ed. Ruth Calder [Geneva: Droz, 1970], p. 200), an alternate reading of lines 142–43. We cite the English translation by J. M. Cohen, *Gargantua and Pantagruel* (Harmondsworth: Penguin Books, 1955), p. 112.

[22] Jones, "Marcolf the Trickster"; Camille, *Image on the Edge,* p. 26 and illustration 15 on p. 34.

GgI.1, the reader finds this Marcolfian grumble against the utility of sententious wisdom: "'Al to late, al to late / Wan the deth is at the ȝate,' Quod Marcol."[23] Evidence for Marcolf's existence survives at the very edges of English medieval art and literature, but his appearances there are consistent in their pragmatic, survival-oriented, antiauthoritarian stance.

The English priest John Audelay wrote a series of poems c. 1410–26, one of which adopts the voice of Marcolf the "fool" as a vehicle for some sharp criticism of church and state.[24] Richard Firth Green notes that Audelay cites the ominous English proverb, "Be war or ye be wo," in contexts that recall its politically charged use in the letters of John Ball and his followers during the Rising of 1381.[25] The fifteenth-century English poet John Lydgate refers to Marcolf in two of his poems. In "The Order of Fools," Lydgate hails Marcolf as "foundour, patroun, & president" of the order; in the final stanza of "The Debate of the Horse, Goose, and Sheep," he deplores "Fals supplantyng clymbyng vp of foolis, / Vnto chaires of worldly dygnyte, / . . . Marcolff to sitt in Salamonis see ['seat']."[26]

Finally, although it does not mention Solomon or Marcolf, it is worth noting among the traces of the Marcolfian tradition in England an anonymous Middle English poem preserved in British Library MS Harley 541, fols. 212r–213r, in a hand dated to the first half of the fifteenth century.[27] In a dialogue between two allegorical personifications that represent nature (Kynd) and training or upbringing (Nurtur), Kynd supports its claims to override Nurtur through a variety of arguments that culminate in the same "cat and the candle" demonstration employed to the same persuasive end by Marcolf in our *Dialogue* (13.1–8). As Braekman and Macaulay note, the word *nurtur* suggests a possible source in Latin for the Middle English poem, and it is of course possible that the source was a version of the Latin *Dialogue*. One variation of the poem's refrain, "I preve that kynde passis nurture" (line 28), corresponds quite closely to Marcolf's statement, "coram te probavi plus valere naturam quam nutrituram," 13.5 ("I proved before you that nature is more influential than nurture"). In the Latin manuscripts of the *Dialogue* that circulated in the first half of the fifteenth century when this poem was written down, Solomon restrains his well-trained cat from chasing a mouse with a variety of sounds or gestures, depending on the manuscript: a grunt (*grunitu*), a groan (*gemitu*), or a shout (*clamore*), as Benary's apparatus indicates. In the Middle English poem, Nurtur, the Solomonic figure who stands for a proper upbringing, restrains the cat by speaking to it, apparently by name: "'What, Nyce,' quoth Nurtur, 'com do thi cure'" (line 58). Whether the author of the English "Kynd and Nurtur" poem had encountered a version of *The Dialogue of Solomon and Marcolf* remains an open question, but clearly the poem shares one of the *Dialogue*'s main themes, the contest between a Solomonic belief in the lasting effects of moral training and a Marcolfian

---

[23] Ziolkowski (*Solomon and Marcolf*, pp. 354–55) reproduces the opening section of the Harley 2253 text, where the reference to "Marcolf's son" occurs in line 3. The Harley text and Cambridge University Library MS GgI.1 are edited by Gustav Schleich, "Die Sprichwörter Hendings und die Prouerbis of Wysdom," *Anglia* 51 (1927), 220–77.

[24] Audelay, *Poems and Carols*, ed. Fein, pp. 32–64; *Poems of John Audelay*, ed. Whiting, pp. 10–46.

[25] Green, "Marcolf the Fool," pp. 569–70.

[26] Lydgate, *Minor Poems*, "The Order of Fools" appears on pp. 449–55 (citation of line 5), "The Debate of the Horse, Goose, and Sheep" on pp. 539–66 (citation of lines 604–05, 608).

[27] For the dating and a text of the poem, see Braekman and Macaulay, "Story of the Cat and the Candle in Middle English Literature."

insistence that the best of training can be overcome by the power of instinct, appetite, and bodily necessity.

5. STRUCTURE AND CONTENTS

Varying views of the dialogue's structure have been offered by scholars working from Benary's 1914 edition based on the Würzburg manuscript of 1434. Most place considerable emphasis on the major break between the end of the long, minimally framed exchange of proverbial remarks and the rest of the work, in which the narrative framing is much more extensive. The English text marks this break with a space, a slightly larger initial, and a new opening formula, "Onys upon a tyme" (6.1). The contrast in the amount of narrative framing and other inconsistencies between these two parts have led scholars to posit that different authors composed them.[28] While no conclusive evidence survives about the work's evolution over time, it is doubtless true that at least two and probably more "authors" played a role in the composition of the surviving versions. Another source of variation is the incorporation of preexisting materials that differ widely in age and origin: proverbs, riddles, antifeminist screeds, folktale motifs, borrowings from biblical wisdom literature.

Many scholars follow Benary in the belief that only the first part of the work merits the designation "dialogue," a position which led him to title his edition *Salomon et Marcolfus*, in preference to the traditional Latin title, *Dialogus Salomonis et Marcolfi*. In our view, the dialogic nature of the work is not limited to the long exchange of proverbs, and thus we retain here the title *The Dialogue of Solomon and Marcolf*, following the practice of the printed editions, where the title *Dialogus* or *Collationes* (*Conversations*) is applied to the whole work. Helen Cooper aptly characterizes it as a framing tale, an analogue of Boccaccio's *Decameron* and Chaucer's *Canterbury Tales*.[29] Although the *Dialogue* frames verbal contests rather than tales within an overarching narrative, this model offers a more dynamic and unified view of the structure than the oft-applied description of a "dialogue proper" followed by a narrative sequel.

The entire work can be read as a sustained dialogue in the form of five verbal contests set into a narrative frame.[30] Each of the five verbal competitions makes use of a different rhetorical form: genealogies, proverbs, riddles, arguable propositions, and arguments on both sides of an issue (*argumentum in utramque partem*). Not just in the proverb contest but throughout the work, King Solomon, avatar of spiritual authority and worldly power, competes largely by citing his own sonorous injunctions from the Old Testament, while the quick-witted peasant Marcolf uses his powers of improvisation to undermine or overturn nearly every statement made by the king. Solomon's utterances derive from his moral wisdom (*sapiencia*); Marcolf improvises by the seat of his pants (sometimes almost literally), relying on his inventive and amoral cleverness. Solomon's *sapiencia* is thus challenged by a rival mental quality called *ingenium* (8.17, 8.20, 12.20) and *versucia* (7.1, 7.6) in the Latin print and rendered in English as "wyt" (8.17, 8.20), "wysedom and subtyltye" (7.1), "subtiltie" (7.6), and "crafte and subtyltye" (12.20).

---

[28] Ziolkowski, *Solomon and Marcolf*, pp. 11–12.

[29] Cooper, "Sources and Analogues of Chaucer's *Canterbury Tales*," esp. pp. 202–04.

[30] Bradbury, "Rival Wisdom."

A brief opening scene introduces Solomon, king of Jerusalem, at whose court Marcolf arrives from the east. Marcolf's appearance is "greatly myshapen and fowle," but he is nevertheless "right talkatyf, elloquend and wyse." His still less attractive wife accompanies him, though later in the surviving versions of the work, Marcolf resides at home with his parents and siblings with no mention of a wife. Medieval peasants were frequently depicted as coarse-featured and were regularly compared to animals,[31] and in these caricatured physical portraits, Marcolf and his wife share certain of their features with those of horses, goats, asses, swine, and bears.

The first verbal contest (4.1a–4.2c) takes the form of rival genealogies. Solomon demands that this ungainly pair inform him of their lineage, presumably a disconcerting question to put to peasants, but Marcolf shrewdly insists that Solomon reveal his own lineage first. Solomon recounts the twelve generations of patriarchs recorded in scripture, ending with the assertion that "David gat Salomon the king, and that am I" (4.2a). Solomon's list of "begats" gives Marcolf a framework on which to hang his own ragtag genealogy and that of this wife, Polycana. Marcolf announces that he descends from twelve generations of "chorlys" ('churls'), the first of which was called "Rusticus," in Latin a rural man or peasant. The Latin names of his other ancestors suggest images of crops and wine dregs.[32] The English Polycana lays claim to a more wholesome background than her Latin equivalents, who, even in the relatively sanitized Latin prints, descend from twelve generations of *lupicanae* ('whores,' but also by etymology 'she-wolves'). In the English text, on the whole more genially comic and less virulently antifeminist than its Latin predecessors, she descends from twelve generations of "untydy wyves" (4.2c).

The exchange of genealogies has the feel of a qualifying round, and Marcolf apparently remains competitive because Solomon now challenges him to an "altercacion" (4.3a), or formal academic disputation. Although Solomon asserts that he will question and Marcolf will answer, in fact what ensues is a long series of exchanges in which Solomon most often utters a sententious moral statement from the Old Testament wisdom books, to which Marcolf responds by transposing the thought into common or vulgar language, applying it to barnyard animals, asserting the opposite position, or upending Solomon's utterance in some other way, with results that vary from parodic mocking to trenchant commentary. Often it is up to the reader to decide whether the pairing amounts to simple arse-baring irreverence on Marcolf's part or sharp-edged social commentary.

As an instance of the former, Solomon states that out of the abundance of the heart, the mouth speaks, and Marcolf replies that out of a full belly the arsehole trumpets ("Out of a full wombe th'ars trompyth," 4.71b). These lexical substitutions — the belly for the heart and anus for the mouth — are typical of Marcolf's verbal play in the proverb contest. In Bakhtin's words, Marcolf "degrades" Solomon's wisdom by transposing it to "the lower stratum of the body, the life of the belly and the reproductive organs; it therefore relates to acts of defecation and copulation, conception, pregnancy, and birth."[33] To "degrade" Solomon's wisdom is thus to make it dirtier and uglier but also to give it a fertile new life for medieval and early modern audiences. As an example of an exchange that offers social commentary, Solomon urges that humans comfort ourselves against the knowledge of our

---

[31] Freedman, *Images of the Medieval Peasant*, pp. 139–53.

[32] Marini, *Il dialogo di Salomone e Marcolfo*, p. 140n8.

[33] Bakhtin, *Rabelais*, p. 21.

mortality by feasting while we can, "Lete us ete and drinke; we shall alle deye." Marcolf responds, "The hungery dyeth as wele as the full fedd" (4.56ab). When Marcolf speaks for the poor and powerless, the bite in some of these exchanges can be very sharp.

The remaining verbal contests — the exchanges of riddles, the posing and proving of arguable propositions, and the production of arguments on both sides of the same issue — are more deeply embedded in narrative framing. They extend and complicate the ideological points raised in the proverb contest, but each follows that contest's essential pattern: the king's established authority (verbal, political, and religious) is continually challenged by the sharp-tongued peasant's verbal cleverness and unmatched improvisational skills.

For the third verbal contest, the exchange of riddles, the scene moves from Solomon's court to Marcolf's peasant house. The change of venue reveals that Marcolf may be a grotesque outsider at the court, but he has his own place: a hearth and a home with a plot of land around it. On his own turf, it is Marcolf who initiates the contest and sets the form his competition with Solomon will take. King Solomon displays considerably less expertise in riddling than in wielding genealogies or proverbs, perhaps because most of Marcolf's riddles require experiential knowledge of peasant life. For example, Marcolf makes the riddling statement that his father is out in the field where he "makyth of oon harme two" (6.11). Questioned by Solomon about what this means, Marcolf explains that his father sets out thorn bushes as a barrier to those who have beaten a path through his fields, with the result that the trespassers trample even more crops as they create a second, equally harmful path (6.16). Although Marcolf makes an unconventional wisdom figure, his riddles concern the very basics of premodern human life: childbearing, the cultivation and cooking of food, the struggle against vermin, and the last attentions to the dead. That Solomon is incapable of solving these riddles suggests that his wisdom alone is incomplete; it does not respond to the whole range of human needs.

As he leaves Marcolf's house, Solomon unwisely poses an agricultural riddle of his own, asking Marcolf for a pot of milk "coveryd" by the same cow (8.2–3). Marcolf's capable mother, Floscemya, has no difficulty with this riddling directive. She milks their cow and covers the container with a flan also made from its milk (in Latin the edible solution is a *placenta* or cake "whitened" or glazed with milk). Marcolf's incessant hunger inspires him to an alternative solution: he gets the better of Solomon by eating the flan and substituting for it another product of the same cow, a "drye bakyn cowe torde" (8.9).

When the gift is presented to the startled king, who was expecting the flan as a cover, Marcolf justifiably points out that his solution answers equally well to the verbal requirements of the riddle. As Marcolf explains, "Sic factum fuit, sed fames mutavit ingenium," which might be translated, "That's how it was done, but hunger changed my stratagem" (or "my plan" or "my mind") (8.17). Perhaps in order to preserve the stress on Marcolf's most salient quality, his *ingenium*, the English translator gives, "So was it furste done, but hungyr chaungyd wyt." The transformational effect of bodily need on "wyt" — on cleverness, perception, and survival skills — is an important theme of the whole work, as is also evident from the etiological tale Marcolf tells in 7.1–10 of how Solomon got his moral wisdom (*sapiencia*) by eating a vulture's heart prepared by his mother. The leftover crust that Solomon's mother throws at the hungry young Marcolf's head gives him the crafty, survivalist cleverness (Latin *versucia*, Middle English *subtiltie*) that keeps him ahead of his rival. In the riddling contest, then, Solomon's high clerical wisdom proves inadequate to a practical, experience-based battle of wits. As the outwitted king later observes, "Marcolph, thou doost alle thy thynges by crafte and subtyltye" (12.20).

The fourth and fifth verbal competitions are more closely related to academic disputation than the earlier contests in genealogies, proverbs, and riddles. The fourth competition is in fact a contest-within-a-contest, its outer layer a waking contest on which Solomon sets a capital penalty: Marcolf must stay awake all night or pay with his head. As the night passes, Solomon repeatedly accuses Marcolf of sleeping, and each time Marcolf utters a proposition as evidence that he is thinking and musing, not sleeping. The model for this tongue-in-cheek verbal contest may be the form of debate that medieval academic disputants inherited from Aristotle, in which one participant posed a "yes or no" question — Is the world eternal or not? — and then tried to compel a second participant to agree with his chosen position.[34] Marcolf's first three propositions are rather inconsequential, apparently intended to parody the topics of scholastic disputation: "I thinke that there are as many joyntys in the tayle of an hare as in hire chyne ('chine' or 'backbone')"; "I thynke that the pye ('magpie') hath as many whyte fethrys as blacke"; "I thinke that undre th'erthe is no clerer thing than the daye" (9.4–10). Much more is at stake in the final two propositions: "I muse how that men may not surely truste the women" and "I thinke how that nature goth afore lernyng" (9.14–16). In each case, Solomon demands that Marcolf prove his assertion, again on pain of death.

Although the connection to medieval disputation might lead us to expect parodic logical proofs, in fact Marcolf demonstrates all his claims empirically, the first two by laying hold of a hare and a magpie and counting the relevant bones and feathers, the last three by cleverly plotted stratagems, each more elaborate than the last. Marcolf proves that daylight is "clerer" — that is, 'brighter' or 'whiter' than milk — by arranging for the king to stumble over a pan of milk in the darkness and nearly break his neck, as Solomon fumes afterward. To prove that women cannot keep their word, Marcolf uses infuriating insults and invented threats of disinheritance to goad his sister Fudasa into revealing a secret she promised faithfully to keep.

The final and most telling proof of this contest is Marcolf's demonstration that nature overrides nurture (Latin *nutritura* 'upbringing, training, education'; the Middle English word is *lerning*). Here the work's medieval author or authors drew upon the internationally distributed folktale of the cat and the candle for yet another demonstration of Marcolf's cleverness. As noted in our discussion of Marcolf above, in this version of an intriguing tale, thought to be of Middle Eastern origin, Solomon has trained his cat to hold a burning candle at the table, and Marcolf comes to supper with three mice up his sleeve, releasing them one at a time until the cat's nature overrides its training, and it takes off after the third mouse. Marcolf declares victory, "Here I have now provyd before you that nature goth afore lernyng" (13.5). Marcolf's conclusion is consistent with his insistence throughout the dialogue that bodily necessity, instinct, and appetite override abstract moral precepts and other forms of training or 'lerning.'

The form at play in the fifth and final verbal contest reflects the practice described by medieval rhetoricians as argument *in utramque partem* ('on both sides of an issue') and draws also on the display form of rhetoric used in composing extravagant speeches of praise or blame. This last verbal contest is the most richly embedded of the five in the dialogue's

---

[34] Stump, *Dialectic and Its Place in the Development of Medieval Logic*, pp. 12–14.

narrative frame. Here, Solomon makes a speech in lavish praise of women, much of it drawn from the description of the good woman in the biblical book of Proverbs that was attributed to Solomon in the Middle Ages. Marcolf initiates the last challenge by promising to see to it that Solomon will soon blame women as strongly as he has praised them. Toward this end, Marcolf improvises an ambitious fiction that begins by disrupting Solomon's most famous judgment (18.3) and succeeds in inciting the women of Solomon's kingdom to rise up against him and revile him to his face. Their false accusations (based on misinformation from Marcolf) and their open defiance move Solomon to an antifeminist tirade, also drawn largely from the biblical wisdom books medieval readers attributed to him. Having successfully led Solomon into self-contradiction, Marcolf once again proclaims verbal victory: "Now have ye spokyn aftyr myn intent. . . . alwayes ye make my saying trewe" (22.5–6).

The narrative frame into which these verbal contests are set recounts various jests perpetrated by Marcolf, and most of them hinge on verbal quibbles. Two such quibbles end the work, one a final and literal instance of gratuitous arse-baring and one a matter of Marcolf's survival. At the beginning of the dialogue, Marcolf and his wife were caricatured by comparisons to animals. Over the course of the work, the exercise of Marcolf's wit gradually turns this kinship with the animal world from an aspersion to an advantage: he uses a hare concealed beneath his shirt to distract the hounds Solomon's courtiers turn on him, and he uses the mice up his sleeve to prove his proposition about the dominance of natural instinct over learned behavior. Marcolf's willingness to expose the animal under his human clothing resonates with the many animal images he evokes throughout the proverb contest and provides a consistent means of throwing Solomon off balance. Infuriated by the trouble Marcolf has stirred up among the women of his kingdom, the king orders him off with the fervent wish that he never see Marcolf again. Solomon phrases his wish rather awkwardly — he never wishes to see the peasant again *in mediis oculis* or "betwixt the yes ('eyes')" (22.9). Ever elaborate in his fictions and ruses, after a fresh snowfall Marcolf takes a sieve and a bear paw, reverses his shoes, and goes "lyke a beste upon alle fowre feet through the strete" to an outdoor oven (24.3–4), a common feature of medieval towns. With his men Solomon tracks the prints of this strange beast, only to find Marcolf, "hys vysage from hymwardes," who has "put downe hys breche into hys hammes" so that Solomon "myght se hys arshole and alle hys othre fowle gere." When Solomon asks what he is doing, Marcolf reminds Solomon of his wording, "Now and ye woll not se me betwyxt myn yes, ye may se me betwene my buttockys in the myddes of myn arsehole" (24.8–12).

For Solomon, this disconcerting reminder of the animal body concealed beneath human clothing is the final straw, and he condemns Marcolf to hang. Marcolf instantly requests that he choose his own tree, a request Solomon grants without thinking; it doesn't matter to him which tree Marcolf hangs from. Marcolf searches far and wide but is somehow unable to find any tree from which he would choose to hang. In Benary's manuscript-based text, Marcolf escapes from this particular scrape, as he has from others, and the work simply ends there — Ziolkowski aptly describes this abrupt halt as "the opposite of closure."[35] Our printed texts, however, both Latin and English, bring the wanderer to rest and the frame narrative to a close. Marcolf returns to his house to live *in pace* in the Latin text and, in Middle English, "in pease and joye" (25.7). The Middle English text adds a brief prayer for salvation, asking

[35] Ziolkowski, *Solomon and Marcolf*, p. 6.

that, just as Marcolf has found lasting contentment, so may the author and the readers find peace and joy after death: "And so mote we alle do aboven wyth the Fadre of Heven. Amen" (25.8), a conventional way to end even the most secular of medieval narratives.

6. TEXTUAL HISTORY

a. Prehistory

The prehistory of *The Dialogue of Solomon and Marcolf* extends from the time of the biblical accounts, when the first recorded challengers to Solomon's wisdom began to appear, and continues until the first known written text appears in the early 1400s. Within this long time span, the period from about 1160 to 1230 stands out as particularly important to the work's gradual formation. Insofar as the narrative frame evokes historical and social realities, the setting seems most consistent with the late twelfth and early thirteenth centuries.[36] In this period most scholarship took its energy from dialectic, a method of reasoning and argumentation that required one scholar to forward an arguable proposition and a second scholar to refute it or to argue a counterproposition. Through arguing contrary propositions, scholars sought to reach a level of truth higher than that represented by either proposition alone. The argumentative energy that animated medieval scholarship spilled over into European vernacular literature in the period c. 1160–1230, creating what Constance Brittain Bouchard has called a "discourse of opposites"[37] that fostered the creation and popularity of dialogues such as the one presented here between a king and a peasant, the opposite poles of medieval political and social life.

Writers of the late twelfth and early thirteenth centuries seem to have been more intrigued or amused than scandalized by Marcolf's rival wisdom. Around 1165, the troubadour Raimbaut d'Orange (or d'Aurenga) wrote a highly cryptic love poem that implies that his lady's pronouncements (*ditz*) are more worthy of attention than those of Solomon or Marcolf.[38] In the 1180s, William, bishop of Tyre, alludes to an account of Marcolf, "of whom it is said that he solved Solomon's riddles (*enigmata*) and responded by proposing equally difficult riddles to be solved by him in turn."[39] William's word *enigmata* could apply to the challenges the two interlocutors set one another in the proverb contest, and a proverb could itself be called an *enigma*, but if, as is more likely, *enigmata* means "riddles," it is notable that Solomon and Marcolf also set riddles to one another in the surviving versions (6.1–8.20).

Given that the earliest allusions most often seem to refer to the long proverb contest that takes up most of the surviving work's first half, it may be that this section preserves the *Dialogue*'s oldest part. Writing c. 1000, Notker of St. Gall states that "Marcolf struggles against the proverbs of Solomon"; in c. 1230, the Swabian poet Freidank reports that

---

[36] Marini, "La dissacrazione come strumento di affermazione ideologica."

[37] Bouchard, *"Every Valley Shall Be Exalted."* For further scholarship on oppositions, contraries, and contradictions in twelfth- and thirteenth-century literature, see Gravdal, *Vilain and Courtois*; Solterer, *Master and Minerva*; Brown, *Contrary Things*; and Kay, *Courtly Contradictions*.

[38] Raimbaut, *Life and Works*, ed. Pattison, pp. 78–80.

[39] William of Tyre, *Chronicon*, ed. Huygens 13.1, p. 586. For translation and commentary, see Ziolkowski, *Solomon and Marcolf*, pp. 334–37.

"Solomon taught wisdom, Marolt subverted (or 'overturned') it."[40] Those who consult Benary's manuscript-based edition will find that in about a fifth of the total number of proverb exchanges (about twenty-eight by our count), Marcolf replies not with a different saying drawn from medieval proverb tradition but rather with a very close verbal parody of Solomon's utterance, as in these examples:

B 132ab	Salomon:	Bene decet gladius honestus juxta latus meum.
	Marcolfus:	Bene decet strontus juxta sepem meam.
	[Solomon:	Very fitting is a fine sword next to my flank.
	Marcolf:	Very fitting is a turd next to my hedge.]
B 138ab	Salomon:	Benefac justo et invenies retribucionem magnam; et si non ab ipso, certe a Domino. (Ecclesiasticus 12:2)
	Marcolf:	Benefac ventri et invenies eructuacionem magnam; et si non ab ore, certe a culo.
	[Solomon:	Do good to the just, and you shall find great recompense, and if not of him, assuredly of the Lord.
	Marcolf:	Do good to the belly, and you shall find great belching, and if not of the mouth, assuredly of the arsehole.]

Although we do not know the dialogue's early history, exchanges of this type — Solomonic pronouncement mocked by close verbal parody — may have formed the work's original clandestine core, whether oral or written. As Bakhtin has shown, medieval scholars engaged in irreverent verbal play of this sort when they composed Latin masses for drunkards or for braying asses. *The Dialogue of Solomon and Marcolf* may have begun with a similar activity and in a similar spirit: in the second example above, as in many other cases, Solomon's words echo scripture, and thus Marcolf's reply parodies sacred language. The proverb contest may well be the oldest part, but we know very little about how the work evolved over time, and when we consider the age of its various parts, it is worth keeping in mind the point made above: as early as the 1180s, William of Tyre seems to connect Solomon and Marcolf to the posing and solving of riddles. Robert J. Menner observes that the riddling section of the *Dialogue* (6.1-8.20 in our texts) could also preserve material that is very old, "inherited ultimately from the early Solomonic riddle-contests."[41] All we can say with certainty about the relative age of the parts of the *Dialogue* is that most of its Solomonic wisdom goes back to biblical times while most of Marcolf's contributions arise from the Middle Ages.

---

[40] For texts, translations, and commentary, see Ziolkowski, *Solomon and Marcolf*, pp. 318, 348.

[41] Menner, ed., *Poetical Dialogues of Solomon and Saturn*, p. 27.

b. Manuscripts

About twenty-seven surviving manuscripts[42] transmit recognizable versions of the Latin *Dialogue* as we have come to know it. Although the earliest manuscript (Benary's U; Griese's *D*) is dated to 1410, it consists of a mere nine proverb exchanges, some of which correspond to exchanges from the proverb contest in the fullest manuscripts, while other exchanges have been cobbled together from episodes occurring later in the work as it survives in those more extensive manuscript versions. All the extant manuscripts of the *Dialogue* date to the fifteenth century and nearly all of them were copied in southern Germany or Austria, which attests to the *Dialogue*'s particular popularity in German-speaking lands.[43] Sixteen of these manuscripts transmit a "long" version of the text, presenting all five verbal contests: (1) rival genealogies, (2) dueling proverbs with about 138 exchanges, (3) riddles, (4) arguable propositions (e.g., "I think nature is more influential than nurture"), (5) arguments "on both sides of an issue." (See section 5 above for an account of these contests.) These sixteen manuscripts fall into two families of eight (Benary's x and y), the latter differing from the former principally in having some proverbs transposed in predictable ways. Benary chose as his base text Würzburg, Universitätsbibliothek M.ch.f. 65, fols. 62r–77v (dated 1434 at fol. 174r), which he regarded as the best witness in the strongest family of manuscripts, family x. Würzburg 65 (Benary's C; Griese's *Wü*) is written in a clear, legible hand, and the copyist has taken great care in making his transcription. It has fewer obvious mistakes than other manuscripts, and the quality of the text is high throughout.

The remaining eleven manuscripts constitute a strikingly heterogeneous third family (Benary's z). These manuscripts all transmit a truncated version of the *Dialogue*, omitting substantial portions of the proverb contest and, in some cases, whole episodes from the narrative frame or whole verbal contests. Some manuscripts in this group contain texts of the *Dialogue* that have been so freely reworked that it is no longer meaningful to speak of manuscript variants pertaining to a single text; rather, they constitute alternative versions. The form in which late medieval readers experienced the dialogue between Solomon and Marcolf depended very much on which manuscript or printed version came into their hands.

c. The Printed Editions

Although the earliest manuscript dates from c. 1410, most of the surviving manuscripts of the *Dialogue* appear to have been copied in the second half of the fifteenth century. Of the forty-nine extant Latin printed editions of the *Dialogue*, about thirty-eight were published between c. 1473 and c. 1515. Whereas the majority of manuscripts were copied in southern Germany and Austria, the majority of printed editions were produced in northern Germany

---

[42] The *Dialogue*'s original editor, Walter Benary, had twenty-two manuscripts, of which nineteen contained a version of the *Dialogue* close to the one we know. Four manuscripts from eastern Germany and Poland have since disappeared. Griese (*Salomon und Markolf*, pp. 31–59) has identified eight manuscripts unknown to Benary and our own research has uncovered one more previously unknown manuscript: Vienna, Dominikanerkloster Cod. 30, fols. 76r–93v. Benary's discussion of the manuscript tradition and his textual notes are both indispensable, but the formatting of the notes makes them difficult to follow. Ziolkowski provides a fuller and much clearer presentation, *Solomon and Marcolf*, pp. 250–83.

[43] Griese, *Salomon und Markolf*, p. 59.

and the Low Countries.[44] The Latin printed editions are normally preceded by one of two titles, either *Dialogus Salomonis et Marcolfi* or some version of the more prolix *Collationes quas dicuntur fecisse mutuo rex Salomon sapientissimus et Marcolphus facie deformis et turpissimus tamen ut fertur eloquentissimus feliciter* ("Conversations that are said to have been conducted by the most wise King Solomon and Marcolf, who, though very ugly and ill-shapen, was, as is said, very clever and quick of speech"). The Latin printed editions contain all five of the verbal contests that make up the "long" manuscripts, but they include only about eighty-nine of the 138 proverb exchanges. In this respect, the Latin printed editions are more or less uniform. However, they do not always print the same text. Initially, not even the relative fixity that came with printing could tame the *Dialogue*'s protean nature. In the first decade of printed editions (c. 1473–c. 1483), the work was issued with the *Dialogus* title (or with no title) and a text that Walter Benary designated as δ. Around 1483, however, the work began to be printed with the longer *Collationes* title and a new text with slightly different readings. Benary designated this text as δ[1].

Based upon a small sample of prints, Benary concluded that the titles were reliable indicators of the text printed.[45] That is, he assumed all prints with the *Dialogus* title would contain the text he designated as δ, while all prints with the *Collationes* title would contain the δ[1] text, and this conclusion has been accepted by subsequent scholars, including Griese in her valuable catalogue of the *Dialogue*'s known Latin printed editions.[46] Benary regarded his conclusion as provisional, and indeed it needs to be revised and corrected by a more thorough examination of the surviving printed texts. For example, the Latin text we print in this volume is entitled *Salomonis et Marcolphi Dyalogus*, but it has the δ[1] text associated by Benary with the *Collationes* tradition. We think it likely that after c. 1483 all Latin printed editions of the *Dialogue* had the δ[1] text, irrespective of title (*Dialogus* vs. *Collationes*). Our conclusion is based on inspection of the twelve printed editions (six entitled *Dialogus*, six entitled *Collationes*) currently shelved in the university libraries at Oxford and Cambridge. Of the six with the *Dialogus* title, the two published prior to c. 1483 have the δ text, while the four published after c. 1483 all have the δ[1] text.[47] All six with the *Collationes* title also have the δ[1] text.[48] On the basis of this evidence, we infer that after c. 1483 the *Dialogue* began to be printed with the new δ[1] text, normally preceded by the lengthy *Collationes* title, but that some printers issued the new δ[1] text with the *Dialogus* title, perhaps because the work had become familiar under that name.

Both texts presented in this volume issued from the printing presses of Gerard Leeu, and thus it is worth outlining briefly what is known of the career of this talented craftsman and shrewd businessman. One of the most important fifteenth-century printers in the Low Countries, Leeu first practiced his craft in his hometown of Gouda (1477–84), where he produced the splendid *Dialogus Creaturarum*, with over 120 expressive and witty woodcuts featuring animals.[49] In 1484, he moved his business to Antwerp, a thriving commercial

---

[44] Griese, *Salomon und Markolf*, p. 65.

[45] Benary, ed., *Salomon et Marcolfus*, pp. xxix–xxx.

[46] Griese, *Salomon und Markolf*, pp. 59–65.

[47] Griese, *Salomon und Markolf*, p. 62, nos. 1, 4, 6, 8, 10, 12.

[48] Griese, *Salomon und Markolf*, pp. 63–64, nos. 6, 7, 10, 11, 12, 18.

[49] L. Hellinga, "*Dialogus creaturarum moralisatus.*" pp. 91–95.

center with a "magnetic attraction for printers,"[50] where he worked until his death in December of 1492. Like other entrepreneurially-minded printers, he saw the advantages of working in a large trading town with better access to credit and to foreign markets, including the English trade. One of the earliest surviving advertisements for a book in Dutch is his 1491 broadsheet promoting a new edition of the romance of Melusine, featuring a titillating woodcut image of the half-serpent Melusine in the bath with her husband observing her unaware.[51]

Trade between London and Antwerp flourished in the late medieval period, and Leeu soon recognized the commercial potential of the English market. He first published a grammar and some liturgical books for English speakers between about 1486 and 1491, and then in 1492 and 1493, his four works wholly in English appeared: a reprint of Caxton's 1477 translation of *The History of Jason*, a reprint of Caxton's 1485 translation of the French romance *Paris and Vienne*, a print (or reprint?) of the otherwise unknown Middle English *Dialogue of Solomon and Marcolf*, and, finally, a reprint of Caxton's *Chronicles of England*, an English work that Caxton printed in 1480 and again in 1482.[52] It was while printing *The Chronicles of England*, in December of 1492, that Leeu died as a result of a quarrel with his talented type cutter, Henric van Symmen. According to a statement by the sheriff of Antwerp, van Symmen "wished to work on his own account"; apparently he had shown interest in setting up his own business.[53] Their disagreement turned violent, Leeu suffered a head wound, and he died two or three days later. The colophon to the *Chronicles* serves as a poignant epitaph for its printer; it suggests that Leeu's laborers felt the loss of a good master: "Enprentyd by maistir Gerard de Leew, a man of grete wysedom in all maner of kunnyng : whych nowe is come from lyfe unto the deth, whiche is grete harme for many a poure man."[54]

Leeu printed the Middle English text of the *Dialogue* presented here in 1492, and thus it numbers among the earliest books to be printed in our language. The title page displays a woodcut (figure 3) depicting the two participants in the ensuing dialogue, as well as Marcolf's wife, Polycana, also mentioned in the early pages of the text. Above the woodcut is the announcement, "This is the dyalogus or communyng betwxt [*sic*] the wyse king Salomon and Marcolphus." The book's incipit or opening summary expands and varies the title: "Here begynneth the dyalogus or comynicacion betwixt Salomon the king of Jherusalem and Marcolphus that right rude and great of body was but right subtyll and wyse of wyt and full of undrestandyng." On the final page, the colophon identifies the printer: "Emprentyd at Andewerpe by me M. Gerard Leeu."

No one knows why only one printed copy of the Middle English *Dialogue* survives, nor is it possible to estimate how many have disappeared. Fifteenth-century print runs averaged somewhere around 250 to 275, but they could vary from an exceptional low of forty-five copies for a book printed for private distribution to highs of several thousand for a standard religious

---

[50] W. Hellinga, *Copy and Print in the Netherlands*, p. 13.

[51] Hirsch, *Printing, Selling and Reading*, p. 64n9, citing Schorbach, "Eine Buchanzeige," p. 139. Schorbach reproduces the Melusine image.

[52] For a bibliography of Caxton's printed works, see Blake, "William Caxton," pp. 57–63.

[53] W. Hellinga and L. Hellinga, *Fifteenth-Century Printing Types*, 1:73. *The Chronicles of England* was printed in 1493; its colophon attests that Leeu was already dead when it appeared.

[54] Duff, ed., *Dialogue or Communing*, pp. xxiii–xxiv, quotation at p. xxiv.

work — runs of 400 were not unusual by 1470.[55] Entire print runs could of course be destroyed through fire, water damage, shipwreck, or other disasters prior to distribution. Some scholars take a single survival to indicate that the book was "read to pieces"; others take it to indicate lack of interest. Little can be deduced about a work's popularity from a lone survival.

Nothing is known about the identity of the English translator whose text Leeu published in 1492. Three of Leeu's four books wholly in English derive from William Caxton's press. Two of these were translated by Caxton himself (the evidence comes from Caxton's own testimony);[56] another, *The Chronicles of England*, was printed by Caxton from a source already in English. Given Leeu's reliance on Caxton's work, Duff judged it "improbable" but possible that Caxton also translated the Middle English *Dialogue of Solomon and Marcolf* (probably the third to be printed of Leeu's books wholly in English, followed by the *Chronicle*).[57] Beecher rules out Caxton as translator of the English *Dialogue* on the grounds that Caxton left the Low Countries for England in 1476, "a date too early for him to have had at his disposal a version of the printed Latin text corresponding to the English version," that is, "Leeu's Latin edition" of c. 1488.[58] However, the flow of merchants and books between London and the Low Countries in this period was so steady that Caxton's relocation to England need not have prevented him from acquiring books printed by Leeu. According to N. F. Blake, Caxton used Leeu's 1479 edition of a Dutch prose version of *Renard the Fox* as the basis for his 1481 translation of that work into English;[59] if so, then Caxton did have continued access to Leeu's books after he moved his press to England in 1476. Still, no tangible evidence connects our English text to Caxton or to any other translator.

In addition to working from a Latin original, our English translator may also have consulted a Dutch translation, since there are clear affinities between the English translation and the only surviving Dutch translation, published in Antwerp in 1501 by Henrik van Homberch. Willem de Vreese investigated these affinities in his 1941 edition of the Dutch translation, *Dat dyalogus of twisprake tusschen den wisen coninck Salomon ende Marcolphus* (a close equivalent of the title given to Leeu's Middle English text). Most striking is the prayer each translator attaches to the end of the dialogue. Unlike the manuscript versions, which tend to break off after Marcolf cleverly eludes Solomon's death sentence, the Latin printed versions usually end with Marcolf returning home to live in peace ("Et sic evasit manus regis Salomonis. Post hoc domum remeans quievit in pace," 25.7). To this ending, the English and Dutch translations both attach a conventional prayer not present in any Latin version known to us:

> English: "And so mote we alle do aboven wyth the Fadre of Heven. Amen." (25.8)
> Dutch: "Ghelijc wij moeten alle gader hier boven metten hemelschen vader. Amen."

Similarly, both translators choose not to translate closely the four lines of poetry that follow the description of Marcolf's wife at 3.1–6. Though obviously misogynistic, the exact meaning

---

[55] Hirsch, *Printing, Selling and Reading*, p. 15 (including n9) and pp. 66–68.

[56] Blake, ed., *Caxton's Own Prose*, pp. 103, 128.

[57] Duff, ed., *Dialogue or Communing*, p. xxiii.

[58] Beecher, ed., *Dialogue of Solomon and Marcolphus*, p. 85.

[59] Blake, ed., *History of Reynard the Fox*, p. xx.

of the verse is obscure. Each translator opts for conveying its gist in two sentences introduced by the expression "That is to say":

> English: "That is to saye, an evyll favouryd and a fowle blacke wyf behovyth to shewe the dayes lyght. It is to oure yes medycyne to se that fayre is and fyne."
> Dutch: "Dat is te segghen, Een eyeselijc wijf leelick ende swart behoort te schouwen des daghes lichte. Tis onsen ogen medecijn te sien dat schoon is ende fijn."

The correspondence between these remarks can hardly be coincidental.

Other correspondences noted by Vreese corroborate the clear evidence just cited that the two translations are related.[60] Either the Dutch translator in 1501 consulted the 1492 English translation or both consulted a lost text produced prior to 1492 that contained their common readings. The possibility that the Dutch translator simply translated the English into Dutch without consulting the original Latin can be ruled out, since the Dutch translation contains errors that do not derive from the English. When Marcolf says that he thinks the hare has as many joints in its tail as in its spine ("quot in spina," 9.4), the English translator gets it right ("as in hire chyne ['backbone']"), whereas the Dutch translator has "as in an ear of corn" ("alst sijn in een aere van koorne"), apparently reading *spica* for *spina* in his Latin text. Vreese assumed that, since most printed editions of the *Dialogue*, both Latin and vernacular, were produced in Germany and the Low Countries, the work would have been translated into Dutch before it was translated into English. He hypothesized that Leeu may have been induced by the success of an earlier Dutch translation, now lost, to commission the 1492 English translation. Both translations, English and Dutch, contain errors, some of which are identical, but the Dutch contains errors not present in the English. Hence, Vreese's hypothesis about a lost Dutch original, which both translators had consulted. The 1501 Dutch edition was, he surmised, to be regarded as a "sloppy reprint" ("slordige nadruk") that introduced errors not present in its original.[61]

Given the state of the evidence, it is not possible to determine the precise affiliation between the two translations. What seems clear is that both translators worked from a Latin text (or texts) and that one or both of them also sought help from a vernacular translation. A prudent translator might well consult more than one text, since the *Dialogue* presents the reader with quite a few obscure or corrupted passages of Latin. If we allow for the omissions, additions, and reworkings characteristic of medieval translation, the Middle English text provides the reader with a reasonably accurate and faithful version of Leeu's 1488 Latin print, whatever the actual source text or texts used by its translator. As our explanatory notes indicate, the tendency that most individuates the English translation is that it goes even further than the other abridgments in replacing mordant satire and exhibitionist scatology with milder, jollier comedy.

7. BRIEF OVERVIEW OF SCHOLARSHIP

The reader in search of more information about the *Dialogue* can do no better than to start with Jan M. Ziolkowski's *Solomon and Marcolf*, with its accessible version of Walter

---

[60] Vreese and de Vries, eds., *Dat dyalogus of twisprake*, pp. 40–47.

[61] Vreese and de Vries, eds., *Dat dyalogus of twisprake*, p. 44.

Benary's manuscript-based Latin text, accompanied by a modern English translation, extensive commentary, appendices that include a translated Welsh version of the dialogue, and nearly thirty pages of bibliography. Also wide-ranging yet accessible is Donald Beecher's *Dialogue of Solomon and Marcolphus* (1995), which offers Leeu's English printed text in facsimile, facing a modernized English transcription, with a long introduction, commentary, and an English translation of a 1497 German Solomon and Marcolf play by Hans Folz. Beecher gives special attention to the English text and to Marcolf's impact on late medieval and early modern literature in English. An overview of the Middle English work is provided by Francis Lee Utley in "Dialogues, Debates, and Catechisms" (1972). Sabine Griese offers a valuable and compact account of the vast textual tradition in *Salomon und Markolf* (1999). An attractive little book, now rare but still worth consulting, is E. Gordon Duff's 1892 volume, *The Dialogue or Communing between the Wise King Salomon and Marcolphus*, with its emphasis on the importance of the work in the history of English printing. Duff reproduces a facsimile of the print with a diplomatic transcription.

To give only a skeletal guide to literary interpretation, an excellent place to begin might be Mikhail Bakhtin's *Rabelais and His World*. Bakhtin mentions the Latin dialogue only in passing, but his influential theories of carnivalesque laughter, popular-festive forms, and especially images of the "material bodily lower stratum" serve as valuable guides to Marcolf's means of mocking and resisting authority. Enid Welsford's 1935 study, *The Fool: His Social and Literary History*, follows early scholarship in regarding Marcolf as a "mythical" figure descended from gods and demons but gives a shrewd account of his role in the Latin dialogue, anticipating scholarship in the Bakhtinian vein: "Marcolf, though frankly a buffoon, is also a sage in his own peculiar way, and even in some respects a greater sage than Solomon; for he represents practical sense as against theoretical idealism, the dispute . . . between the upper and lower classes of this world."[62] Natalie Zemon Davis's "Proverbial Wisdom and Popular Errors" (1975) also presents the work as a dialogue between peasant practicality and an idealism that is too exclusionary to hold a monopoly on wisdom and truth.

Maria Corti's structuralist reading of 1979, "Models and Antimodels in Medieval Culture," wields enormous binary oppositions in a way that resembles the medieval dialogue itself. It thus lacks historical nuance, but it is a stimulating essay that identifies Marcolf with the medieval authors who struggled against biblical and clerical authority, resisting their canonical predecessors and yet seeking to appropriate their authority. Quinto Marini responds to Corti in an equally illuminating and much more historically situated essay, "La dissacrazione come strumento di affermazione ideologica" (1987); he has also edited a dual text edition, *Il dialogo di Salomone e Marcolfo* (1991), that parallels Benary's manuscript-based text with that of a Venetian printed edition of 1502. In "Rival Wisdom in the Latin *Dialogue of Solomon and Marcolf*" (2008), Nancy Mason Bradbury argues for the unity of the Latin dialogue in pitting static clerical learning against improvisational wit and experiential knowledge throughout.

Two very substantial articles on the visual images belonging to this tradition are Malcolm Jones, "Marcolf the Trickster in Late Mediaeval Art and Literature or: The Mystery of the Bum in the Oven" (1991), and Michael Curschmann, "Marcolf or Aesop? The Question of Identity in Visio-Verbal Contexts" (2000), while a 2002 article by Jan M.

---

[62] Welsford, *Fool: His Social and Literary History*, p. 39.

Ziolkowski ("The Deeds of Aesop and Marcolf") complements the Curschmann essay by drawing out further parallels between Marcolf and Aesop. Richard Firth Green's 2001 article, "Marcolf the Fool and Blind John Audelay," presents compactly the evidence for interest in Marcolf in late medieval England, including the "Marcolf" poem of the fifteenth-century English writer John Audelay. James Simpson, "Saving Satire after Arundel's *Constitutions*: John Audelay's 'Marcol and Solomon'" (2005), argues that Audelay's poem shows knowledge of *Piers Plowman*. The debate about Audelay's sources continues in two essays in a collection edited by Susanna Fein, *My Wyl and My Wrytyng* (2009), one by Richard Firth Green and one by Derek Pearsall. Recent work on Caxton's career includes *Caxton's Trace* (2006), a collection of essays edited by William Kuskin, and a monograph by the same author, *Symbolic Caxton: Literary Culture and Print Capitalism* (2008). For a comprehensive introduction to early English printing, see *The Cambridge History of the Book in Britain*, vol. 3: *1400–1557*, ed. Lotte Hellinga and J. B. Trapp.

A Note on the Latin and Middle English Texts

The anonymous Middle English (ME) text derives from the single surviving copy of Gerard Leeu's edition, printed in Antwerp in 1492, and preserved in the Bodleian Library, Oxford, under the shelfmark Tanner 178 (3). It appears in the second edition of the *Short Title Catalogue* (no. 22905) under the title *This is the dyalogus or co[m]munyng betwxt [sic] the wyse king Salomon and Marcolphus*. Facsimiles of the ME print are available in the editions by E. Gordon Duff and Donald Beecher and through Early English Books Online (http://eebo .chadwyck.com).

The Latin text presented here is one of four surviving copies of Gerard Leeu's edition, printed in Antwerp c. 1488 under the title *Salomonis et Marcolfi Dyalogus*. The copy transcribed is preserved in the university library at Cambridge under the shelfmark Inc. 5.F.6.2 (Oates 3913).

In keeping with the editorial practices of METS, we have regularized spellings in *i/j* and *u/v*, added *–e* to *the* when the ME pronoun *thee* is meant, and followed modern rules of capitalization, punctuation, and word division, adding an apostrophe in ME contractions such as *th'este* ('the east') and *th'erthe* ('the earth'). The numbering of the texts is our own. In square brackets in our Latin text, preceded by B (Benary), we provide the headings and numbering from Walter Benary's 1914 edition. These "Benary numbers" are essential for comparing the texts of the prints to Benary's manuscript-based edition and locating citations from previous scholarship.

We have silently expanded abbreviations, including the names of the two speakers, except in sections 4.4a to 4.91b (the proverb contest), where we designate the rapidly alternating speakers by S (Salomon) and M (Marcolph). Elsewhere we expand the abbreviations *M, Mar, Marc*, and *Marcol* to *Marcolph* in ME (the most common spelling of the name in the English text) and to *Marcolphus* in Latin. In the ME text, we preserve the variants on the full spelling of "Marcolph": it appears as *Marcolphus* (either spelled out in full or with a stroke to indicate "*-us*"), *Marcolfus* (again both spelled out and with the "*-us*" abbreviated), and *Marcolf*. We treat "Maccolph," "Marcolpus," "Marcof," and "Marcoph" as typographical errors.

Typographical errors are silently corrected in the text and listed in the Textual Notes at the end of the volume.

Figure 1. *Marcolf.* From *Salomonis et Marcolphi Dyalogus.* Antwerp: Gerard Leeu, c. 1488. Reproduced by permission of the University Library, Cambridge. Shelfmark: Inc. 5.F.6.2, fol. 1r.

Salo.   Os inimici uon loquitur veritatē nec verū labia eꝰ
personabūt Mar.   Qui te nō amat ipse te nō diffamat.
Salo. Quid satis est dozmi. Mar./ Cui licet z non dozmit,
pigritia nocet illi/ Salo.   Sacietate repleti sumus referamus deo grās Marcol.   jubilat merulus respondit gra-
culus/non equalit cātant saturatus z ieiunus Salo. Madu-
cemꝰ z bibem? omēs enim moziemur Mar.   Sic mozif
famelicus sicut z refectus. Salo. Qñ hō harpat nō pt palogisare. Mar.   Qñ canis cacat nō pōt latrare. Salo Saciata est iniqtas ventris nūc eamus dozmitū Mar. Tozmat re-
tozmat male dozmit qui non māducat Salo. Exiguū munus cū dat tibi paup amicus noli despicere Mar. Qō habz castratus dat vicine sue. Salo. Ne gradieris cū hōie malo vel litigioso ne forte senties malū ppter eum vel piculū Mar.
Apis moztua non caccat mel Salo. Si cū hōie callido vel
maliuolo amiciciā firmaveris magi tibi adversabit ꝗ auxilium
pstet. Mar.   Quod lupus facit lupe placet, Salo.
Qui añ rūdit ꝗ audiat stultū se demōstrat. Mar. Quādo
te aliqs pūgit subtrahe pedē tuū Salo: Dē aiāl sile sibi eligit.
Mar. Vbi fuerit caballꝰ scabiosus parē sibi qzit z ytriqz se scabiunt. Salo.   Bñ facit aie sue vbi est hō misericoz Mar.
Magnū donū despicit qui seipm ñ cognoscit Salo. Qui fugit
lupo obviat leoni. Mar. De malo in malū/de coquo ad pis-
tozēm Salo. Caue ne quis faciat tibi malū si autem fecerit noli ei facere. Mar. A que nō currenti z hōi tacenti credere noli:
Salo. Non oēs oia possunt Marcol. Scriptū est in casibus:
quin habz equum vadat pedibꝰ Salo/ Puer centū annozum
maledcūs erit. Mar. Tardē est veterē canē in ligamen mittere. Salo. Modo habenti dabitur z habūdabit Mar.
Ve hōi qui nō hz panes z hz parentes Salo. Ve viro duplici
corde z duabz vijs incedēte Mar. Qui duas vias vult ire aut
culū aut bracā debz rūpe. Salo. Ex habūdātia cordis os loqt
Mar. Ex saturitate ventris triūphat culus Salo. Duo bo-
ues equalit trahūt ad vnū iugū Mar. Due vene equalit vadūt
ad vnū culū Salo. Mulier pulchza est a viro suo amanda.

Figure 2. *Sample of the Proverb Contest.* From *Salomonis et Marcolphi Dyalogus.* Antwerp: Gerard Leeu, c. 1488. Reproduced by permission of the University Library, Cambridge. Shelfmark: Inc. 5.F.6.2, fol. 4r

Figure 3. *Marcolf and his wife, Polycana, before King Solomon.* From *The Dyalogus or Communyg betwixt the wyse King Salomon and Marcolphus.* Antwerp: Gerard Leeu, 1492. Reproduced by permission of the Bodleian Libraries, Oxford. Shelfmark: Tanner 178 (3), fol. 1v.

he that angzely spekyth/beyth evple oz shzewdz
ly/ Mar/   Saye not in thyn angze to thy frende
no evyl/left thou fozthynke it aftrewardz Sak.
The mouthe of an ennemye kan faye no good.
ne hys lyppys shall fownde no trouthe: Mar.he
that lovyth me not/doth not diffame me/ Salo.
Slepe as ye have nede/ Ma/ He that leyth hym
downe to flepe & kan not/is not at hys hertys ea-
fe/ Sal We haue well fyllydz oure belyys lete vs
thanke god?/ Mar/ As the owfell whyftelyth fo
anfweryth the thzuffhe the hũgery and the fulle
fynge not oon fonge/ Sal.Lete vs ete ãd dzinke
we fhall alle deye Marc.   The hũngery dyeth
afwele as the full feddz: As a man playeth vpõ
an harpe he kan not wele îdicte Mar. So whã
the hownde fhytyth he berkyth noth/ Sal:The
wzetchydz wombe is full go we now to bedde.
Marcol. He turnyth and walowyth & flepyth
evyl that hath not foz to ete. Salo.Dyfpyfe thou
not a lytyll yifte that is yeven the of a trewe frẽ
de Mar.That a Geldydz man hath that yevyth
he to his neigbozwes/ Salo/Go thou not wyth
the evyll man oz the bzawelyng:left thou fuffre
evyll foz hym oz peryle Marcolph⁹ A dede bee
makyth no hony/ Salo.If thou make frẽdefhip
with a falfe and evylwylledz man.it fhalhyndze
the moze than pzoffyte: Marcolphus:
What the wolf doth/that pleafyth the wolfeffe
       Salomon: He that anfweryth afoze

Figure 4. *Sample of the Proverb Contest.* From *The Dyalogus or Communyg betwixt the wyse King Salomon and Marcolphus.* Antwerp: Gerard Leeu, 1492. Reproduced by permission of the Bodleian Libraries, Oxford. Shelfmark: Tanner 178 (3), fol. 6r.

SALOMONIS ET MARCOLPHI DYALOGUS

SALOMONIS ET MARCOLPHI DYALOGUS

[B PARS I, PROLOGUS]

1. (1) Cum staret Salomon super solium David patris sui, plenus sapiencia et diviciis, (2) vidit quendam hominem Marcolphum nomine a parte orientis venientem, facie turpissimum et deformem et tamen eloquentissimum. (3) Uxor ejus erat cum eo, que nimis erat terribilis et rustica. (4) Cum eos ambos conspectui suo pariter exhiberi jussisset, stabant ambo ante eum se mutuo conspicientes.

2. (1) Statura itaque Marcolphi fuit brevis et grossa. (2) Caput habuit grande, frontem latissimam, rubicundam et rugosam, aures pilosas et usque ad medium maxillarum pendentes, (3) oculos grossos et lipposos, labium subcominus quasi caballinum, barbam sordidam et setosam quasi hyrci, (4) manus truncas, digitos breves et grossos, pedes rotundos, (5) nasum spissum et gibbosum, labia magna et grossa, faciem azininam, capillos veluti hyrcorum. (6) Calciamenta pedum ejus rustica erant nimis, pannitiosa atque lutosa pellis; (7) curta tunica usque ad nates, calige repagulate, vestimenta ejus coloris turpissimi erant.

3. (1) Uxor quoque ejus erat pusilla et nimis grossa cum mammis grossis. Comam habebat spinosam, (2) supercilia longa, setosa et acuta quasi dorsum porci, barbam ut habet hyrcus, aures asininas, oculos lipposos, aspectum colubrinum, (3) carnem rugosam et nigram, et massa de plumbo ornabat grossas mammas ejus. (4) Digitos habebat breves ornatos anulis ferreis. (5) Nares habebat valde grandes, tibias breves et grossas, in modum urse pilosas; (6) tunica ejus erat pilosa et dirupta. (7) De tali quidem muliere quidam juvenis hos dixit versus:

🦋 THE DIALOGUE OF SOLOMON AND MARCOLF

THIS IS THE DYALOGUS OR COMMUNYNG BETWIXT THE WYSE KING SALOMON AND MARCOLPHUS

Here begynneth the dyalogus or comynicacion betwixt Salomon the king of Jherusalem and Marcolphus that right rude and great of body was but right subtyll and wyse of wyt and full of undrestandyng, as thereafter folowyng men shall here.

1. (1) Upon a season hertofore as King Salomon, full of wisdome and richesse, sate upon the kinges sete or stole that was his fadres Davyd, (2) sawe comyng a man out of th'este that was named Marcolphus, of vysage greatly myshapen and fowle, nevyrthelesse he was right talkatyf, elloquend and wyse. (3) His wif had he wyth hym, whiche was more ferefull and rude to beholde. (4) And as they were bothe comen before King Salomon, he behelde thaym welle.

2. (1) This Marcolf was of short stature and thykke. (2) The hede had he great, a brode forhede rede and fulle of wrinkelys or frouncys, his erys hery and to the myddys of chekys hangyng, (3) great yes and rennyng, his nether lyppe hangyng lyke an horse, a berde harde and fowle lyke unto a goet, (4) the handes short and blockyssh, his fyngres great and thycke, rownde feet, (5) and the nose thycke and croked, a face lyke an asse, and the here of hys heed lyke the heer of a goet. (6) His shoes on his fete were ovyrmoche chorlysh and rude, and his clothys fowle and dyrty; (7) a shorte kote to the buttockys, his hasyn hynge full of wrynkelys and alle his clothes were of the moost fowle coloure.

3. (1) His wyf was of short stature, and she was out of mesure thycke wyth great brestys, and the here of hyr hede clustred lyke thystelys. (2) She had longe wynde browes lyke brostelys of a swyne, longe erys lyke an asse, renning yen, berdyd lyke a goet; (3) hyr vysage and skyn blacke and full of wrynkelys, and upon hyr great brestys she had, of span brode, a broche of leed. (4) She had short fyngres, full of yren ryngys. (5) She had right great nosethrylles, hyr leggys short and hery lyke a bere; (6) hyr clothes were rough and broken. (7) Of suche a woman, or of anothre lyke unto hyre, a yonge man hath made thies verses folowyng:

Prologue 1 rude, coarse. **1.2 th'este**, the east; **vysage,** appearance. **2.2 frouncys**, creases; **erys**, ears; **myddys**, middle. **2.3 yes**, eyes; **nether**, lower. **2.6 ovyrmoche chorlysh and rude**, extremely countrified and rough. **2.7 hasyn**, hose (long stockings). **3.1 thystelys**, thistles. **3.2 wynde**, twisted; **brostelys**, bristles; **erys**, ears; **renning yen**, running eyes. **3.3 of span brode**, of the breadth of a hand with fingers spread; **broche of leed**, brooch or pin of lead. **3.4 yren**, iron. **3.5 nosethrylles,** nostrils.

Femina deformis tenebrarum subdita formis
Cum turpi facie transit absque die.
Est mala res multum turpi concedere cultum,
Sed turpis nimirum turpe ferat vitium.

[B Dialogus]

4. (1a) [R]ex vero Salomon, cum eos conspexisset, sic exorsus est dicens: "Qui estis et unde est genus vestrum?"

(1b) Marcolphus respondit: "Dic tu nobis prius genealogiam tuam et patrum tuorum, et tunc indicabo tibi genus nostrum." [B 1ab]

(2a) Salomon: "Ego sum de duodecim generibus patriarcharum: Judas genuit Phares, Phares genuit Esron, Esron genuit Aram, Ara genuit Aminadab, Aminadab genuit Naazon, Naazon genuit Salmon, Salmon genuit Boos, Boos genuit Obeth, Obeth genuit Isay, Isai genuit David regem, David autem genuit Salomonem, et ego sum Salomon rex."

(2b) Marcolphus respondit: "Ego sum de duodecim generibus rusticorum: Rusticus genuit Rustam, Rusta genuit Rustum, Rustus genuit Rusticellum, Rusticellus genuit Tarcum, Tarcus genuit Tarcol, Tarcol genuit Pharsi, Pharsi genuit Marcuel, Marcuel genuit Marquart, Marquart genuit Marcolphum, et ego sum Marcolphus follus."

(2c) "Uxor vero mea de duodecim generibus lupicanarum: Lupica genuit Lupicanam, Lupicana genuit Ludiprag, Ludiprag genuit Bonestrung, Bonestrung genuit Boledrut, Boledrut genuit Pladrut, Pladrut genuit Lordam, Lorda genuit Curtam, Curta genuit Curtulam, Curtula genuit Curtellam, Curtella genuit Policam, Polica genuit Policanam, et hec est Policana uxor mea." [B 2abc]

(3a) Salomon dixit: "Audivi te esse verbosum et callidum, quamvis sis rusticus et turpis. Quamobrem inter nos habeamus altercationem. Ego vero te interrogabo, tu vero subsequens responde mihi."

(3b) Marcolphus respondit: "Qui male cantat, primo incipiat." [B 3ab]

(4a) S: "Si per omnia poteris respondere sermonibus meis, te ditabo magnis opibus, et nominatissimus eris in regno meo."

(4b) M: "Promittit medicus sanitatem, cum non habet potestatem." [B 4ab]

(5a) S: "Bene judicavi inter duas meretrices, que in una domo oppresserant infantem."

(5b) M: "Ubi sunt aures ibi sunt cause, ubi mulieres ibi parabole." [B 5ab]

(6a) S: "Dominus dedit sapientiam in ore meo, cum nullus sit mihi similis in cunctis finibus terre."

(6b) M: "Qui malos vicinos habet seipsum laudat." [B 6ab]

Femina deformis tenebrarum subdita formis   *(see note)*
Cum turpi facie transit absque die.
Est mala res multum turpi concedere cultum,
Sed turpis nimirum turpe ferat vicium.

(8) That is to saye, an evyll favouryd and a fowle blacke wyf behovyth to shewe the dayes lyght. It is to oure yes medycyne to se that fayre is and fyne.

4. (1a) As Kyng Salomon thies two persones thus had seen and beholden, he demaunded of thaym of whens they weryn and of what lynage they were comyn.

(1b) Marcolphus thereto answeryd: "Saye furste to us youre kynrede and genleagie, and of youre fadres, and than shall I shewe and declare you of oures."

(2a) Salomon: "I am of the xii kyndredes of patryarkes, that is to wete, that Judas gate Phares, Phares gat Esron, Esron gat Aron, Aron genderyd Aminadab, Aminadab gat Naazon, Naazon gat Salmon, Salmon gat Boos, Boos gat Obeth, Obeth gat Ysay, Ysay gat Davyd king, David gat Salomon the king, and that am I."

(2b) Marcolfus answeryd: "I am of the xii kindred of chorlys: Rusticus gat Rustam, Rusta gat Rustum, Rustus gat Rusticellum, Rusticellus gat Tarcum, Tarcus gat Tarcol, Tarcol gat Pharsi, Pharsi gat Marcuel, Marcuel gat Marquat, Marquat gat Marcolphum and that is I.

(2c) "And my wyf is comen of the blood and xii kyndredes of untydy wyves, that is to knowe, of Lupica that gat Lupicana, Lupicana gat Ludibrac, Ludibrac gat Bonestrung, Bonestrung gat Boledrut, Boledrut gat Paldrut, Paldrut gat Lordan, Lordan gat Curta, Curta gat Curtula, Curtula gat Curtella, Curtella gat Polica, Polica gat Polycana, and thys is my wyf Polycana."

(3a) Salomon sayde: "I have herd of thee that thou kanst right wele clatre and speke, and that thou art subtyle of wyt, although that thou be mysshapyn and chorlyssh. Lete us have betwene us altercacion. I shal make questyons to thee, and thou shalt therto answere."

(3b) Marcolphus answeryd: "He that singyth worste begynne furste."

(4a) S: "If thou kanst answere to alle my questyons, I shall make thee ryche, and be named above alle othre withyn my reaume."

(4b) M: "The phisician promysyth the seeke folke helthe, whan he hath no power."

(5a) S: "I have juged betwixt two light women, whiche dwellyd in oon house and forlaye a chylde."

(5b) M: "Were erys are there are causes, where women be there are wordys."

(6a) S: "God yave wysdam in my mouth, for me lyke is none in alle partys of the worlde."

(6b) M: "He that hath evyll neighborys praysyth hymself."

3.8 behovyth to shewe, should avoid (eschew); **yes**, eyes; **that**, that which. **4.1a lynage**, lineage (ancestry). **4.1b kynrede and genleagie**, kindred and genealogy. **4.2a that is to wete**, namely; **gate**, begat; **genderyd**, engendered (begat). **4.2b chorlys,** churls (common men or peasants). **4.2c that is to knowe**, namely. **4.3a clatre**, chatter; **altercacion**, argument, formal disputation. **4.4a reaume**, realm. **4.5a light**, immoral; **forlaye**, suffocated by lying on. **4.5b Were erys are**, Where there are ears; **causes**, points at issue. **4.6a yave**, gave.

(7a)   S: "Fugit impius nemine subsequente."

(7b)   M: "Quando fugit capriolus, albescit ejus culus." [B 7ab]

(8a)   S: "Bona mulier et pulchra ornamentum est viro suo."

(8b)   M: "Olla plena cum lacte bene debet a catto custodiri." [B 8ab]

(9a)   S: "Mulier sapiens edificat sibi domum, insipiens constructam destruit manibus."

(9b)   M: "Olla bene cocta melius durat et qui mundam distemperat mundam bibit." [B 10ab]

(10a)   S: "Mulier timens deum ipsa laudabitur."

(10b)   M: "Cattus cum bona pelle ipse excoriabitur." [B 11ab]

(11a)   S: "Mulier pudica est multum amanda."

(11b)   M: "Lacticinia sunt pauperi retinenda." [B 12ab]

(12a)   S: "Mulierem fortem quis inveniet?"

(12b)   M: "Cattum fidelem super lac quis inveniet?" [B 13ab]

(12c)   S: "Nullus."

(12d)   M: "Et mulierem raro." [B 13cd]

(13a)   S: "Mulier formosa et honesta retinenda est super omnia desiderabilia bona."

(13b)   M: "Mulier pinguis et grossa est largior in dando visa." [B 14ab]

(14a)   S: "Bene peplum album in capite mulieris."

(14b)   M: "Scriptum est enim, 'Non sunt talia manice quales pellicia; sub albo peplo sepe latet tinea.'" [B 16ab]

(15a)   S: "Qui seminat iniquitatem metet mala."

(15b)   M: "Qui seminat paleas metet miserias." [B 17ab]

(16a)   S: "Doctrina et sapientia debet in ore sanctorum consistere."

(16b)   M: "Asellus semper debet esse ubi se pascit, ibi crescit. Ubi pascit unam plantam, quadraginta resumit; ubi caccat ibi fimat; ubi mingit ibi rigat; ubi se volvit frangit glebas." [B 19ab]

(17a)   S: "Laudet te alienus."

(17b)   M: "Si meipsum vituperavero, nulli unquam placebo." [B 20ab]

(18a)   S: "Multum mel ne comedas."

(18b)   M: "Qui apes castrat, digitum suum lingit." [B 23ab]

(19a)   S: "In malivolam animam non intrabit spiritus sapientie."

(19b)   M: "In lignum durum dum mittis cuneum, cave ne incidat in oculum." [B 24ab]

(7a) S: "The wykkyd man fleyth, no man folwyng."

(7b) M: "Whan the kydde rennyth, men may se his ars."

(8a) S: "A good wyf and a fayre is to hir husbonde a pleasure."

(8b) M: "A potfull of mylke muste be kept wele from the katte."

(9a) S: "A wyse woman byldeth an house, and she that unwyse and a fool is, distroyeth with hir handes that she fyndeth made."

(9b) M: "A pot that is wele baken may best endure, and that clene is browyn that may they fayre drinken."

(10a) S: "A ferdefull woman shal be praysed."

(10b) M: "A catte that hath a good skyn shal be flayne."

(11a) S: "A shamefast wyf and a fayre is mekyll to be belovyd."

(11b) M: "To pore men whyte mete are to be kept."

(12a) S: "A woman stronge in doyng good, who shall fynde?"

(12b) M: "Who shal fynde a catte trewe in kepyng mylke?"

(12c) S: "Noon."

(12d) M: "And a woman seldom."

(13a) S: "A fayre woman and an honest is to be praysed above alle rychesse that a man fynde may."

(13b) M: "A fat woman and a great is larger in yevyng than othre."

(14a) S: "A whyt kerchyf becomth wele a womans hede."

(14b) M: "It standyth wryten that the furre is not all lyke the slevys, and undre a whyte cloth often are hyd mothys."

(15a) S: "He that sowyth wyckydnesse shal repe evyll."

(15b) M: "He that sowyth chaf shal porely mowe."

(16a) S: "Out of the mouth of a holy man shal come good lernyng and wysedom."

(16b) M: "The asse behovyth to be allweye where he fedyth, for ther it growyth. Where he etyth oon gres, there growe xl ayen; where he dungyth, there it fattyth; where he pyssyth, there makyth he wete; and where he wallowyth, there brekyth he the strawe."

(17a) S: "Lete an othre preyse thee."

(17b) M: "Yf I shulde myself dyspreyse, no man shall I please."

(18a) S: "Thou shalt ete moche ony."

(18b) M: "That beys dryve lykke faste theyre fyngres."

(19a) S: "In an evylle wylled herte the spyryt of wysedome shalle not entre."

(19b) M: "As ye smyte wyth an axe in an hard tre, beware that the chippes falle not in youre ye."

4.7a fleyth, flees. **4.7b kydde,** kid (young goat or deer); **rennyth,** runs; **ars,** arse (hindquarters). **4.9b that clene is browyn,** that which is brewed in cleanliness; **fayre drinken,** drink well. **4.10a ferdefull,** reverent. **4.10b flayne,** flayed (skinned). **4.11a shamefast,** modest; **mekyll,** greatly. **4.13b larger in yevyng,** more generous in giving. **4.15b chaf,** infertile husks of grain. **4.16b behovyth to be allweye,** should always be; **fedyth,** feeds; **ther it growyth,** there [his fodder] grows; **etyth oon gres,** eats one blade of grass; **ayen,** again; **it fattyth,** [the soil] grows richer. **4.17a preyse,** praise. **4.18a ony,** honey. **4.18b That beys dryve,** Those who drive (tend) bees. **4.19b youre ye,** your eye.

(20a)   S: "Durum est tibi contra stimulum recalcitrare."

(20b)   M: "Bos recalcitrosus pungi debet vicibus binis." [B 25ab]

(21a)   S: "Erudi filium tuum et ab infantia doce eum benefacere."

(21b)   M: "Qui suam nutrit vaccam, de lacte sepe manducat." [B 35ab]

(22a)   S: "Omne genus ad suam naturam revertitur."

(22b)   M: "Mappa digesta revertitur ad stuppam." [B 37ab]

(23a)   S: "Quicquid novit loquitur judex justicie et veritatis."

(23b)   M: "Episcopus tacens efficitur hostiarius." [B 39ab]

(24a)   S: "Honor exhibendus est magistro, et virga timenda."

(24b)   M: "Qui suo judici solet ungere buccam, solet macerare suam azellam." [B 41ab]

(25a)   S: "Contra hominem fortem et potentem et aquam currentem noli contendere."

(25b)   M: "Vultur excoriat duram volucrem deplumatque pellem." [B 43ab]

(26a)   S: "Emendemus in melius quod ignoranter peccavimus."

(26b)   M: "Quando culum tergis nil aliud agis." [B 44ab]

(27a)   S: "Blandis persuasionibus noli decipere quenquam."

(27b)   M: "Per ingenium manducat qui manducantem salutat." [B 45ab]

(28a)   S: "Cum homine litigioso non habeas societatem."

(28b)   M: "Merito hunc manducant sues, qui se miscet inter furfures." [B 47ab]

(29a)   S: "Multi sunt qui verecundiam habere nesciunt."

(29b)   M: "Vivunt cum hominibus qui similes sunt canibus." [B 49ab]

(30a)   S: "Multi sunt qui benefacientibus reddunt mala pro bonis."

(30b)   M: "Qui alieno cani panem suum dederit, mercedem non habebit." [B 50ab]

(31a)   S: "Non est amicus qui non durat in amicicia."

(31b)   M: "Merda de vitulo non diu fimat." [B 51ab]

(32a)   S: "Occasiones multas querit qui ab amico recedere velit."

(32b)   M: "Mulier que non vult consentire dicit se scabiosum culum habere." [B 52ab]

(33a)   S: "Sermo regis debet esse immutabilis."

(33b)   M: "Cito tedium habet qui cum lupo arat." [B 53ab]

(34a)   S: "Radices raphani bone sunt in convivio, fetent in consilio."

(34b)   M: "Qui raphanum manducat, ex utraque parte tussit." [B 54ab]

(35a)   S: "Perit auditus, ubi non vigilat sensus."

(35b)   M: "Perdit suam sagittam qui tripum sagittat." [B 56ab]

(36a)   S: "Qui avertit aurem suam a clamore pauperum, ipse clamabit et dominus deus non exaudiet vocem suam."

(36b)   M: "Perdit lachrimas suas qui coram judice plorat." [B 57ab]

(20a) S: "It is hard to spurne ayenst the sharp prykyl."

(20b) M: "The ox that drawyth bacwarde shal be twyse prycked."

(21a) S: "Fede up youre children and from thayre youthe lerne thaym to do welle."

(21b) M: "He that fedyth well his cowe etyth often of the mylke."

(22a) S: "All maner kyndes turne ayen to theyre furste nature."

(22b) M: "A worne tabyllcloth turnyth ayen to his furste kynde."

(23a) S: "What the juge knowyth of right and trouthe that spekyth he out."

(23b) M: "A bisshop that spekyth not is made a porter of a yate."

(24a) S: "Honoure is to be yeven to the maistre, and the rodde to be feryd."

(24b) M: "He that is wonte to anointe the juges handes oftyn tymes he makyth his asse lene."

(25a) S: "Ayenst a stronge and myghty man thou shalt not fyghte, ne stryve ayenst the streme."

(25b) M: "The vultier takyth the skyn of stronge fowles and makyth thaym neked of theyre fethres."

(26a) S: "Lete us amende us in good that unwythyngly we have mysdone."

(26b) M: "As a man wypyth his ars he doth nothing ellys."

(27a) S: "Wyl thou not disceyve any man wyth fayre word?"

(27b) M: "By wyt he etyth that gretyth the ether."

(28a) S: "Wyth brawlyng people holde no companye."

(28b) M: "It is reson that he of the swyne ete that medlyth amonge the bren."

(29a) S: "There be many that kan have no shame."

(29b) M: "They lyve undre the men that are lyke to howndes."

(30a) S: "There are many that to theyr good doers do evyl for good."

(30b) M: "He that yevyth bred to anothre manys hownde shall have no thanke."

(31a) S: "It is no frende that dureyth not in frendeshyp."

(31b) M: "The dung of a calf stynkyth not longe."

(32a) S: "He sekyth many occasions that wolle departe from his maister."

(32b) M: "A woman that wolle not consente seyth that she hath a skabbyd arse."

(33a) S: "A kynges worde shulde be unchaungeable or stedfaste."

(33b) M: "He is sone wery that plowyth wyth a wolf."

(34a) S: "The radissh rotys are good mete but they stynke in the counsell."

(34b) M: "He that etyth radyssh rotys coughyth above and undyr."

(35a) S: "It is lost that is spokyn afore people that undrestande not what they here."

(35b) M: "He lesyth his shafte that shetyth in the sande."

(36a) S: "He that stoppyth his erys from the crying of the pore people, oure Lord God shall not here hym."

(36b) M: "He that wepyth afore a juge lesyth his terys."

4.20a spurne, kick; **prykyl**, goad. **4.21a lerne**, teach. **4.22b his**, its. **4.23b yate**, gate. **4.24a yeven**, given; **feryd**, feared. **4.24b wonte**, accustomed; **asse**, ass (the pack animal). **4.25b vultier**, vulture. **4.26a unwythyngly**, unwittingly (unknowingly). **4.26b As,** When; **ars**, arse; **ellys**, else. **4.27b By wyt he etyth that gretyth the ether**, By his wits he eats who greets another person. **4.28b reson**, fitting; **bren**, bran. **4.30b yevyth bred**, gives bread; **manys**, man's. **4.31a dureyth not**, does not endure (persist). **4.34a radissh rotys**, radish roots; **mete**, food; **counsell**, council. **4.35b lesyth**, loses; **shetyth**, shoots [an arrow]. **4.36a erys**, ears. **4.36b lesyth**, loses (wastes).

(37a)   S: "Surge, aquilo, et veni, auster, perfla ortum meum, et fluent aromata illius."
(37b)   M: "Quando fluit aquilo, ruit alta domus,
            Et qui habet hirnia non est bene sanus." [B 58ab]
(38a)   S: "Mortem et paupertatem celare noli."
(38b)   M: "Cui celat hirniam, crescunt ibi majora." [B 59ab]
(39a)   S: "Cum sederis ad mensam divitis, diligenter inspice que apponantur tibi."
(39b)   M: "Universa ministratio per ventrem dirigitur et in ventrem vadit." [B 63ab]
(40a)   S: "Quando ad mensam sederis, cave ne prius comedas!"
(40b)   M: "Qui in altiori sella sederit, ipse primum locum tenet." [B 64ab]
(41a)   S: "Si fortis supervicerit imbecillem, universam substantiam aufert ejus domus."
(41b)   M: "Bene videt cattus cui barbam lingit voluntariam." [B 65ab]
(42a)   S: "Quod timet impius veniet super eum."
(42b)   M: "Qui male facit et bene sperat, totum se fallit." [B 67ab]
(43a)   S: "Propter frigus piger arare noluit; mendicabit autem et nil dabitur ei."
(43b)   M: "Nudum culum nemo spoliabit." [B 68ab]
(44a)   S: "Studium reddit magistrum benivolum."
(44b)   M: "Assuete manus currunt ad caldarium." [B 73ab]
(45a)   S: "Projiciendi sunt a consortio bonorum litigiosi et garruli."
(45b)   M: "Domina irata, fumus, et ratta, patella perforata damnum sunt in casa." [B
            75ab]
(46a)   S: "Pro amore dei omnis dilectio est adhibenda."
(46b)   M: "Si amas illum qui te non amat, perdis amorem tuum." [B 79ab]
(47a)   S: "Ne dicas amico tuo 'vade, cras dabo tibi', cum statim possis sibi dare."
(47b)   M: "'Ad tempus faciam' dicit qui non habet aptum utensile." [B 80ab]
(48a)   S: "Crapulatus a vino non servat tempus in eloquio."
(48b)   M: "Culus confractus non habet dominum." [B 82ab]
(49a)   S: "Multi concupiscunt divicias habere, cum sint in paupertate detenti."
(49b)   M: "Prande quod habes, et vide quid remaneat." [B 83ab]
(50a)   S: "Multi sunt qui famem sustinent et tamen sustinent uxores."
(50b)   M: "Miser homo panem non habebat, et tamen canem sibi comparabat." [B
            84ab]

(37a)   S: "Ryse up, thou northren wynde, and come forth, thou southren wynde, and blowe through my gardeyne, and the wele smellyng herbys shalle growe and multiplie."

(37b)   M: "Whanne the northren wyndes blowe, than ben the high howses in great trouble and daunger."

(38a)   S: "The deth nor povertye wyll not be hyd."

(38b)   M: "A man that is brostyn and hyde it, they growe the more."

(39a)   S: "As thou syttyst at a riche mans table, beholde diligently what comyth afore thee."

(39b)   M: "Alle metys that is ordeyned for the body muste through the bely, and it goth in the stomak."

(40a)   S: "Whan thou syttyst at the tabyll, beware that thou taste not furst."

(40b)   M: "He that syttyth in the hyghest sete, he holdyth the uppermost place."

(41a)   S: "As the stronge the weyke wynneth, he takyth all that he hath."

(41b)   M: "The catte seeth wele whoos berde she lycke shall."

(42a)   S: "That the wycked feryth, that fallyth hym often."

(42b)   M: "He that doth evylle and hopyth good is disceyvyd in thaym bothe."

(43a)   S: "For the colde the slouthfull wolde not go to plough; he beggyd his brede, and no man wolde hym yeve."

(43b)   M: "A nakyd ars no man kan robbe or dispoyle."

(44a)   S: "Studye makyth a maystre wele wylled."

(44b)   M: "Th'andys that are usyd in the fyre fere not the ketylle."

(45a)   S: "Brawlers and janglers are to be kaste out of alle good companye."

(45b)   M: "An angry howsewyf, the smoke, the ratte, and a broken plater are often tymes unprofytable in an howse."

(46a)   S: "For Goddys love men are bownden to love othre."

(46b)   M: "If thou love hym that lovyth not thee, thou lesyth thyn love."

(47a)   S: "Saye not to thy frende, 'Come tomorowe, I shal yeve thee,' that thou maiste forthwyth yeve hym."

(47b)   M: "He sayth an othre tyme he shalle doo it, that hath noth wherwyth redy for to do it withalle."

(48a)   S: "He that is wyne dronken holdyth nothing that he sayth."

(48b)   M: "An opyn arse hath no lord."

(49a)   S: "Many coveyte to have rychesse that with povertye are holden undre."

(49b)   M: "Ete that ye have, and se what shall remaigne."

(50a)   S: "There are many that susteyne hungyr, and yet fede they theyre wyves."

(50b)   M: "The pore had ne breed and yet he bought an hownde."

4.37b than ben, then are. **4.38b is brostyn**, is ruptured (has hernias). **4.39b metys**, food; **ordeyned**, intended. **4.42a That the wycked feryth**, What the wicked man fears; **fallyth**, befalls. **4.43a brede**, bread; **wolde hym yeve**, would give [it] to him. **4.44a maystre**, (school)master; **wele wylled**, well disposed. **4.44b Th'andys**, The hands. **4.45a janglers**, gossips (chatterers). **4.46a othre**, one another. **4.46b lesyth**, lose (waste). **4.47a I shal yeve thee**, I will give [it] to you [then]; **that thou maiste forthwyth yeve hym**, what you can give him right away. **4.47b wherwyth**, resources; **withalle**, immediately. **4.48a holdyth**, remembers (holds to). **4.50b pore**, poor man; **ne breed**, no bread.

(51a)   S: "Stultus respondit secundum suam stulticiam, ne videatur sapiens."

(51b)   M: "Petra quid audivit, cui respondit quercus." [B 85ab]

(52a)   S: "Ira non habet misericordiam, et ideo qui per iram loquitur, comparat malum seu perpetrat."

(52b)   M: "Ne dicas amico tuo malum iratus, ne postea peniteas placatus." [B 86ab]

(53a)   S: "Os inimici non loquitur veritatem, nec verum labia ejus personabunt."

(53b)   M: "Qui te non amat, ipse te non diffamat." [B 87ab]

(54a)   S: "Quid satis est dormi."

(54b)   M: "Cui licet et non dormit, pigritia nocet illi." [B 92ab]

(55a)   S: "Sacietate repleti sumus, referamus deo gratias."

(55b)   M: "Jubilat merulus, respondit graculus; non equaliter cantant saturatus et jejunus." [B 93ab]

(56a)   S: "Manducemus et bibemus, omnes enim moriemur."

(56b)   M: "Sic moritur famelicus, sicut et refectus." [B 94ab]

(57a)   S: "Quando homo harpat, non potest palogisare."

(57b)   M: "Quando canis cacat, non potest latrare." [B 95ab]

(58a)   S: "Saciata est iniquitas ventris; nunc eamus dormitum."

(58b)   M: "Tornat, retornat, male dormit, qui non manducat." [B 96ab]

(59a)   S: "Exiguum munus, cum dat tibi pauper amicus, noli despicere."

(59b)   M: "Quod habet castratus dat vicine sue." [B 97ab]

(60a)   S: "Ne gradieris cum homine malo vel litigioso, ne forte senties malum propter eum vel periculum."

(60b)   M: "Apis mortua non caccat mel." [B 99ab]

(61a)   S: "Si cum homine callido vel malivolo amiciciam firmaveris, magis tibi adversabitur quam auxilium prestet."

(61b)   M: "Quod lupus facit, lupe placet." [B 100ab]

(62a)   S: "Qui ante respondit quam audiat, stultum se demonstrat."

(62b)   M: "Quando te aliquis pungit, subtrahe pedem tuum." [B 101ab]

(63a)   S: "Omne animal simile sibi eligit."

(63b)   M: "Ubi fuerit caballus scabiosus parem sibi querit, et utrique se scabiunt." [B 102ab]

(64a)   S: "Benefacit anime sue ubi est homo misericors."

(64b)   M: "Magnum donum despicit qui seipsum non cognoscit." [B 103ab]

(65a)   S: "Qui fugit lupo, obviat leoni."

(65b)   M: "De malo in malum, de coquo ad pistorem." [B 104ab]

(51a) S: "The fole answeryth aftyr hys folisshnes, for that he shulde not be knowyn wyse."

(51b) M: "What the stone heryth, that shalle the oke answere."

(52a) S: "Wrathe hath no mercy, and therefore he that angrely spekyth beyth evyle or shrewdly."

(52b) M: "Saye not in thyn angre to thy frende no evyl, lest thou forthynke it aftreward."

(53a) S: "The mouthe of an ennemye kan saye no good, ne hys lyppys shall sownde no trouthe."

(53b) M: "He that lovyth me not doth not diffame me."

(54a) S: "Slepe as ye have nede."

(54b) M: "He that leyth hym downe to slepe and kan not is not at his hertys ease."

(55a) S: "We have well fyllyd oure bellys, lete us thanke God."

(55b) M: "As the owsell whystelyth, so answeryth the thrusshe; the hungery and the fulle synge not oon songe."

(56a) S: "Lete us ete and drinke; we shall alle deye."

(56b) M: "The hungery dyeth as wele as the full fedd."

(57a) S: "As a man playeth upon an harpe, he kan not wele indicte."

(57b) M: "So whan the hownde shytyth, he berkyth noth."

(58a) S: "The wretchyd wombe is full; go we now to bedde."

(58b) M: "He turnyth and walowyth and slepyth evyl that hath not for to ete."

(59a) S: "Dyspyse thou not a lytyll yifte that is yeven thee of a trewe frende."

(59b) M: "That a geldyd man hath, that yevyth he to his neigborwes."

(60a) S: "Go thou not wyth the evyll man or the brawelyng, lest thou suffre evyll for hym or peryle."

(60b) M: "A dede bee makyth no hony."

(61a) S: "If thou make frendeshipe with a false and evylwylled man, it shal hyndre thee more than proffyte."

(61b) M: "What the wolf doth, that pleasyth the wolfesse."

(62a) S: "He that answeryth afore he is demaundyd shewyth hymself a fole."

(62b) M: "Whan a man tredyth, drawe to you youre fete."

(63a) S: "Evrything chesyth his lyke."

(63b) M: "Where a skabbyd horse is, he sekyth his lyke and eyther of thaym gnappyth othre."

(64a) S: "A mercyfull man doth wele to his sowle."

(64b) M: "He dyspyseth a great yifte that knowyth not hymself."

(65a) S: "He that skapyth the wolf metyth the lyon."

(65b) M: "From evyll into worse, as the cooke to a bakere."

4.51b heryth, hears; **oke**, oak. **4.52a beyth**, is; **shrewdly**, wicked. **4.52b forthynke**, regret. **4.53a ne** nor. **4.55b owsell**, ouzel (a bird); **synge not oon songe,** do not sing the same song. **4.56a deye,** die. **4.57a indicte**, compose or write. **4.57b shytyth**, shits; **berkyth**, barks. **4.58a wombe**, belly. **4.59a yifte that is yeven thee of**, gift that is given to you by. **4.59b geldyd**, castrated; **yevyth**, gives. **4.62a demaundyd**, questioned. **4.63a chesyth**, chooses. **4.63b sekyth**, seeks; **gnappyth othre**, snaps at the other [with its teeth]. **4.65a skapyth**, escapes.

(66a)   S: "Cave ne quis faciat tibi malum; si autem fecerit, noli ei facere."

(66b)   M: "Aque non currenti et homini tacenti credere noli." [B 105ab]

(67a)   S: "Non omnes omnia possunt."

(67b)   M: "Scriptum est in casibus, 'Qui non habet equum, vadat pedibus.'" [B 106ab]

(68a)   S: "Puer centum annorum maledictus erit."

(68b)   M: "Tarde est veterem canem in ligamen mittere." [B 110ab]

(69a)   S: "Modo habenti dabitur et habundabit."

(69b)   M: "Ve homini qui non habet panes et habet parentes." [B 111ab]

(70a)   S: "Ve viro duplici corde et duabus viis incedente."

(70b)   M: "Qui duas vias vult ire, aut culum aut bracam debet rumpere." [B 113ab]

(71a)   S: "Ex habundantia cordis os loquitur."

(71b)   M: "Ex saturitate ventris triumphat culus." [B 116ab]

(72a)   S: "Duo boves equaliter trahunt ad unum jugum."

(72b)   M: "Due vene equaliter vadunt ad unum culum." [B 117ab]

(73a)   S: "Mulier pulchra a viro suo amanda."

(73b)   M: "In collo est alba ut columba, in culo nigra et irsuta ut talpa." [B 118ab]

(74a)   S: "In tribu Juda nimia est cognatio mea, et deus patris mei principem me
          constituit populi sui."

(74b)   M: "Cognosco mappam quia de stuppa facta est." [B 119ab]

(75a)   S: "Necessitas facit hominem justum peccare."

(75b)   M: "Lupus apprehensus et in custodia positus, aut caccat aut mordet." [B
          120ab]

(76a)   S: "Sufficeret michi temperaneus honor, si tantummodo deus universum orbem
          mee ditioni subjugasset."

(76b)   M: "Non tantum datur catulo quantum blanditur sua cauda." [B 122ab]

(77a)   S: "Qui tardus venit ad mensam, suspensus est a cibo."

(77b)   M: "Gluto non currit per totum." [B 123ab]

(78a)   S: "Cum molesta tibi sit uxor tua, ne timeas."

(78b)   M: "Molli bergario lupus non cacat lanam." [B 124ab]

(79a)   S: "Non decent stulto verba composita."

(79b)   M: "Non decet canem sellam portare." [B 126ab]

(80a)   S: "Tunde latera filii tui, dum tenera sint."

(80b)   M: "Qui osculat agnum amat et arietem." [B 127ab]

(81a)   S: "Omnes semite ad unam viam tendunt."

(81b)   M: "Ad culum unum omnes tendunt vene." [B 129ab]

(82a)   S: "A bono homine bona fit mulier."

(82b)   M: "A bono convivio bona fit merda, que calcatur pedibus. Sic et bestiales
          mulieres debent calcari." [B 130ab]

(66a) S: "Ware that no man do thee non evyll; if he do, do it not ayen."

(66b) M: "The stylle standyng watyr and the man that spekyth but lytylle, beleve thaym not."

(67a) S: "We may not alle be lyke."

(67b) M: "It standeth wryten in a boke, 'He that hath no horse muste go on fote.'"

(68a) S: "A chylde of an hundred yere is cursyd."

(68b) M: "It is to late an olde hounde in a bande to lede."

(69a) S: "He that hath, shal be yeven, and shall flowe."

(69b) M: "Woo to that man that hath frendes and no breed."

(70a) S: "Whoo to that man that hath a dowble herte and in bothe weyes wyll wandre."

(70b) M: "He that wolle two weyes go muste eythre his ars or his breche tere."

(71a) S: "Of habundaunce of th'erte the mouth spekyst."

(71b) M: "Out of a full wombe th'ars trompyth."

(72a) S: "Two oxen in one yocke drawen lyke."

(72b) M: "Two veynes go lyke to oon ars."

(73a) S: "A fayre woman is to be lovyd of hire husbande."

(73b) M: "In the necke is she whyte as a dove, and in the ars blacke and derke lyke a molle."

(74a) S: "Out of the generacion of Juda is my moost kyndrede; me the Lord of my fadre hath made governoure ovyr his people."

(74b) M: "I knowe wele a tabylcloth and of what werke it is made."

(75a) S: "Nede makyth a right wyse man to do evyll."

(75b) M: "The wolf that is takyn and set fast, eythre he byteth or shytyth."

(76a) S: "Were it so that God alle the world undre my power had set, it shulde suffyse me."

(76b) M: "Men kan not yeve the katte so moche but that she woll hyr tayle wagge."

(77a) S: "He that late comyth to dyner, his parte is leest in the mete."

(77b) M: "The glouton kan not se or renne al aboute."

(78a) S: "Though it be so that thy wif be sowre, fere hir not."

(78b) M: "The shepherde that wakyth welle, ther shall the wolf no wolle shyte."

(79a) S: "It becomth no foles to speke or to brynge forth any wyse reason."

(79b) M: "It becomyth not a dogge to bere a sadylle."

(80a) S: "Whyles the children are lytyll, reighte theyre lymmes and maners."

(80b) M: "He that kyssyth the lambe lovyth the shepe."

(81a) S: "Alle reyght pathys goon towardes oon weye."

(81b) M: "So done alle the veynes renne towardes the ars."

(82a) S: "Of a good man comth a good wyf."

(82b) M: "Of a good mele comyth a great torde that men wyth theyre fete trede. So muste men also alle the bestyalle wyves trede undre fote."

4.66a Ware, Beware; **do it not ayen,** do not return it [the evil]. **4.68b in a bande,** on a leash. **4.70b eythre,** either; **tere,** tear (v.). **4.71a th'erte,** the heart. **4.71b wombe,** belly; **th'ars trompyth,** the arsehole trumpets. **4.75a Nede,** Need (Necessity). **4.75b eythre he byteth or shytyth,** either he bites or shits. **4.76b yeve,** give. **4.77a mete,** food. **4.78b wakyth,** stays awake; **no wolle shyte,** shit no wool. **4.79b bere a sadylle,** bear a saddle. **4.80a reighte,** right (correct). **4.82b torde,** turd; **wyth theyre fete trede,** tread with their feet; **bestyalle wyves,** bestial wives.

(83a)   S: "Bene decet mulier pulchra juxta virum suum."
(83b)   M: "Bene decet olla plena vino juxta sitientem." [B 131ab]
(84a)   S: "Bene decet gladius honestus juxta latus meum."
(84b)   M: "Bene decet strues juxta sepem meam." [B 132ab]
(85a)   S: "Quanto magnus es, tanto humilis sis in omnibus."
(85b)   M: "Bene equitat qui cum paribus equitat." [B 133ab]
(86a)   S: "Filius sapiens letificat patrem suum, insipiens vero mesticia est matris sue."
(86b)   M: "Non equaliter cantant tristis et letus." [B 136ab]
(87a)   S: "Qui parce seminat parce et metet."
(87b)   M: "Quanto plus gelat, tanto plus stringit." [B 137ab]
(88a)   S: "Omnia fac cum consilio, et post factum non penitebis."
(88b)   M: "Satis est infirmus qui infirmum trahit." [B 139ab]
(89a)   S: "Omnia tempora tempus habent."
(89b)   M: "'Diem hodie, diem cras' dicit bos qui leporem sequitur." [B 140ab]
(90a)   S: "Iam fessus loquendo; requiescamus ergo."
(90b)   M: "Non obmittam loquelam meam." [B 141ab]
(91a)   S: "Non possum amplius."
(91b)   M: "Si non potes, humiliter confitere te victum et da quod promisisti." [B 142ab]

[Epilogus]

5.   (1) Ad hoc Bananyas, filius Joiade, et Zabus, amicus regis, et Adonias, filius Abde, qui erant super tributa dixerunt ad Marcolphum: (2) "Ergo tu ne eris tercius in regno domini nostri. (3) Sed eruentur tibi tui pessimi oculi de tuo vilissimo capite. (4) Nam melius decet te jacere cum ursis domini nostri quam sublimari aliquo honore." (5) Quibus Marcolphus ait: "Quis adheret culo nisi pastelli? Quare rex promisit?" (6) Tunc Venthur et Benadachar, Benesia, Bena, Benanudab, Banthaber, Achinadai, Achimaab, Hommia, Josepus, Semes, et Samer, duodecim prepositi regis dixerunt: (7) "Ut quid iste follus infestat dominum regem nostrum? (8) Cur non magnis colaphis maceratur, aut fustibus convictus eicietur de conspectu domini nostri regis?" (9) Ad hoc rex Salomon ait: "Non ita fiat, sed bene saturatus in pace dimittatur." (10) Tunc Marcolphus recedens ait ad regem: "Satis patior quicquid dixeris. (11) Ego semper dicam, 'Ibi non est rex, ubi non est lex.'"

[B Pars II]

6. [B 1]   (1) [R]ex igitur quadam die cum venatoribus suis et copulis canum de venationum persequutione forte transibat ante hospicium Marcolphi folli, (2) divertit se illuc cum equo suo, et inclinato capite suo sub limine hostii, requirens quis intus esset.

(83a) S: "A fayre wyf becomyth well by hir husband."

(83b) M: "A pot full wyth wyne becomth well by the thrusty."

(84a) S: "Wel becomyth a fayre sworde by my syde."

(84b) M: "Wel becomth my hegge a great hepe of stonys."

(85a) S: "The gretter that ye be, the more meke shulde ye be in alle thyngys."

(85b) M: "He rydyth well that ridyth wyth his felawes."

(86a) S: "The wyse chylde gladyth the fadyr, and the folyssh childe is a sorwe to the modyr."

(86b) M: "They synge not al oon songe, the glad and the sory."

(87a) S: "He that sowyth wyth skaerstye repyth skaersly."

(87b) M: "The more it fryseth, the more it byndeth."

(88a) S: "Do alle thynges by counsell, and thou shalt not aftre forthinke it."

(88b) M: "He is seke ynough that the sekenesse drawyth or folowyth."

(89a) S: "Alle thinges have theyre seasons and tyme."

(89b) M: "'Now daye; tomorwe daye,' sayde the oxe that the hare chacyd."

(90a) S: "I am wery of spekyng; lete us therefore reste."

(90b) M: "Therfore shall not Y leve my clapping."

(91a) S: "I may no more."

(91b) M: "Yf ye maye no more, yelde youreself ovyrcomen and yeve me that ye have promysed."

5. (1) Wyth that spake to Marcolf Hananyas, the sone of Joiade, and Zabus, the kinges frende, and Adonias, the sone of Abde, whiche hadden the charge and governaunce ovyr the kynges tribute, and sayde: (2) "Thou shalt not herefore be the thyrdde in the kingedome of oure soveraigne lord. (3) Men shall rather put bothe thyn worst yen out of thy moost vyle hede, (4) for it becomyth thee bettyr to lye amonge berys than to be exalted to any dignyte or honour." (5) Than Marcolphus sayde: "Wherfor hath the king than promysed?" (6) Than sayde the kinges xii provostes, that is to wyte, Nenthur, Benadachar, Benesya, Bena, Benanides, Banthabar, Athurady, Bominia, Josephus, Semes, and Samer: (7) "Whereto comth this fole, oure soveraign lorde al thus to trouble and mocke? (8) Why dryve ye hym not out wyth stavys of his syghte?" (9) Tho sayde Salomon: "Not so, but yeve hym wele to ete and drinke and lete hym than goo in pease." (10) Tho spak Marcolphus goyng his weye to the king: "I suffre ynough what that ye have sayde. (11) I shall alweyes saye, 'There is no king were no lawe is.'"

6. (1) Onys upon a tyme the king rode an huntyng wyth his hunterys and howndes and fortunyd hym to come by the house of Marcolf, (2) and turnyd

---

4.84b hegge, hedge. **4.86b al oon songe,** the same song. **4.87b fryseth**, freezes; **byndeth**, binds. **4.88a counsell**, consultation; **forthinke**, regret. **4.88b seke**, sick. **4.89b 'Now daye; tomorwe daye,'** probably, 'If not today, then tomorrow' (see explanatory note); **that the hare chacyd**, that chased the hare. **4.90b leve my clapping**, stop my chattering. **4.91b yeve me that**, give me what. **5.2 herefore,** on this account. **5.3 worst yen**, miserable eyes. **5.4 berys**, bears. **5.5 Wherfor**, Why. **5.6 provostes,** administrators; **that is to wyte**, namely. **5.8 Why dryve ye hym not out wyth stavys of his syghte?,** Why don't you drive him from the king's presence with sticks? **5.9 Tho,** Then; **yeve,** give. **5.10 Tho,** Then.

(3) Marcolphus respondit regi: "Intus est homo integer, et dimidius, et caput equi, (4) et quanto plus ascendunt, tanto plus descendunt." (5) Ad hoc Salomon dixit: "Quid est quod dicis?" (6) Marcolphus respondit: "Nam integer ego sum intus sedens, dimidius homo tu es supra equum extra sedens, intus prospiciens inclinatus, (7) caput vero equi caput est tui caballi super quem sedes." (8) Tunc Salomon dixit: "Qui sunt ascendentes et descendentes?"(9) Marcolphus respondit et ait: "Fabe in olla bulientes." (10) Salomon: "Ubi sunt tuus pater et tua mater, tua soror et tuus frater?" (11) Marcolphus: "Pater meus facit in campo de uno damno duo damna, (12) mater mea facit vicine sue quod ei amplius non faciet, (13) frater autem meus extra domum sedens, quicquid invenit, occidit. (14) Soror autem in cubiculo sedens plorat risum annualem." (15) Salomon: "Quid illa significant?" (16) Marcolphus: "Pater meus in campo suo est et semitam per campum transeuntem occupare cupiens, spinas in semitam ponit, et homines venientes scilicet duas vias faciunt nocinas ex una, et ita facit duo damna ex uno. (17) Mater mea vero claudit oculos vicine sue morientis, quod amplius ei non faciet. (18) Frater autem meus extra domum sedens in sole et pelliculas ante tenens, pediclos omnes quos invenit occidit. (19) Soror autem mea preterito anno quendam juvenem adamavit, et inter ludicra, risus, et molles tactus, et basia, (20) quod tunc risit, modo pregnans plorat."

7. [B 2]   (1) Ad hoc Salomon ait: "Unde tibi versucia hec venit?" (2) Marcolphus respondit: "Tempore David patris tui, cum essem infantulus, medici patris tui quadam die peragendis medicinis unum vulturem acceperunt, (3) et cum singula membra necessitatibus expendissent, (4) Bethsabea mater tua cor illius accepit, et super crustam ponens in igne assavit ac tibi comedere dedit, (5) mihique qui tunc in coquina eram, crustam post caput projecit. (6) Ego vero crustam vulture perfusam comedi, et inde, ut spero, versucia mea venit, sicut et tibi pro cordis comestione sapientia." (7) Salomon: "Sic te deus adjuvet! In Gabaa mihi apparuit deus et replevit me sapientia." (8) Marcolphus: "Talis dicitur esse sapiens qui seipsum habet pro stulto." (9) Salomon: "Nonne audivisti quales divicias dedit mihi deus insuper et ipsam sapientiam?" (10) Marcolphus: "Audivi. Scio enim quod ubi vult deus ibi pluit."

hymself thidrewardes wyth his horse and demaunded, wyth his hede inclyned undre the dorre bowe, who was wythinne. (3) Marcolf answeryd to the king: "Wythin is an hool man, and an half, and an horse hede, (4) and the more that they ascende, the more they downe falle." (5) To that spak Solomon: "What menyst thou therwithall?" (6) Tho answeryd Marcolphus: "The hole man is myself syttyng wythin, ye are the half man syttyng wythoute upon youre horse, lokyng in wyth youre hede declyned, (7) and the horse hede is the hede of youre horse that ye sytte on." (8) Than Salomon demaunded of Marcolphus what they were that clymen up and fallyn downe. (9) Marcolph answeryd and sayde: "They are the benys boyllyng in the pott. (10) Salomon: "Where is thy fadyr, thy modyr, thy sustyr, and thy brothyr?" (11) Marcolph: "My fadyr is in the felde and makyth of oon harme two. (12) My modyr is goon and dooth to hir neighborwe that she nevyr more shall do; (13) my brothyr sytting wythoute the house sleyth alle that he fyndeth. (14) My sustyr syttyth in hire chambre and bewepyth that aforetyme she laughyd." (15) Salomon: "What betokenth they?" (16) Marcolph: "My fadyr is in the felde and puttyth or settyth thornys in a footpath, and comyng men they make an othre path therby, and so he makyth of oon harme two. (17) My modyr is goon and closyth the yes of hir neyghborwe deying, the whiche she shall nevyr more do. (18) My brothyr sytting withoute the house in the sonne and lowsyth, and alle that he fyndeth, he sleyth. (19) My sustyr the laste yere lovyd a yonge man and wyth kyssyng, laughing, tastyng, japyng, and playing, (20) she was getyn wyth chylde whereof she now travayllyth, and that now she bewepyth sore."

7.   (1) Salomon: "How comyth to thee alle this wysdome and subtyltye?" (2) Marcolfus: "In the tyme of King David youre fadyr, there was a yonge man his phisician, (3) and as he onys had takyn a vulture for to occupye in his medicins and had takyn therof that was to hym expedyent, (4) so toke youre modyr, Barsebea, the herte and leyde it upon a cruste of breed and rostyd it upon the feyre and yave you the herte to ete, (5) and I thanne beyng in the kechin, she kast at my hede the cruste through moysted wyth th'erte of the vulture, (6) and that ete I and therof, I suppose, is comen to me my subtiltie, lyke as to you is comen by etyng of th'erte wysedom." (7) Salomon: "As verelye God helpe thee! In Gabaa, God appieryd to me and fulfylled me wyth sapience." (8) Marcolphus: "He is holdyn wyse that reputyth hymself a fole." (9) Salomon: "Haste thou not herde what rychesse God hath yevyn me abovyn that wysedome?" (10) Marcolph: "I have herde it, and I knowe well that where God woll, there reynyth it."

6.2 thidrewardes, in that direction; **dorre bowe,** door frame. **6.5 "What menyst thou therwithall?"** "What do you mean by all that?" **6.6 declyned,** bent down. **6.9 benys,** beans. **6.11 makyth of oon harme two,** makes two harms out of one. **6.12 that,** that which. **6.13 wythoute,** outside; **sleyth,** slays. **6.14 bewepyth,** beweeps; **aforetyme,** earlier. **6.15 "What betokenth they?"** "What do those things mean?" **6.17 yes,** eyes; **deying,** dying. **6.18 lowsyth,** delouses [himself]; **sleyth,** slays. **6.19 tastyng,** caressing; **japyng,** joking or flirting. **6.20 travayllyth,** suffers the discomfort of pregnancy. **7.3 onys,** once; **expedyent,** useful for his purpose. **7.4 feyre,** fire; **yave,** gave. **7.5 kechin,** kitchen; **through moysted,** soaked; **th'erte,** the heart. **7.7 Gabaa,** the biblical city of Gibeon. **7.8 reputyth,** acknowledges. **7.9 yevyn,** given. **7.10 woll,** wills; **reynyth it,** it rains.

8. [B 3]   (1) Ad hoc Salomon subridens ait: "Homines mei extra domum me exspectant foris. (2) Non possum amplius tecum stare, sed dic matri tue ut de meliori quam habet vacca mittat mihi ollam plenam lacte, (3) et ipsam ollam cooperiat de eadem vacca, tuque michi eam portes." (4) Marcolphus: "Faciam," inquit. (5) Rex vero Salomon cum ingenti strepitu hominum suorum in Jherusalem veniens in pallacio suo sicut dives et potens dominus receptus. (6) Mater autem Marcolphi, Floscemia nomine, rediens, jussum regis ei patefecit. (7) Tunc Floscemia ollam plenam lactis recipiens et placentam candidam de eodem lacte liniens super ollam posuit, (8) sicque Marcolphum, filium suum, regi transmisit. (9) Marcolphus vero per semitam unius prati incedens et calore estatis estuans vidit basam vacce jacentem, (10) vixque ollam ad terram deponens, placentam comedit, et cum basa vacce ollam contexit. (11) Cumque venisset ante regem ollam tectam cum basa vacce representans, (12) ait rex Salomon: "Cur sic olla cooperta est?" (13) Marcolphus: "Nonne jussisti ut lac vacce de vacca cooperiretur? Et factum est." (14) Salomon: "Non ita fieri precepi." (15) Marcolphus:"Sic intellexeram." (16) Salomon: "Melius fuisset, si placenta lacte fuisset linita." (17) Marcolphus: "Sic factum fuit, sed fames mutavit ingenium." (18) Salomon: "Quomodo?" (19) Marcolphus: "Sciebam te non indigere pane et indigens comedi placentam lacte linitam, (20) et pro ipso ingenio mutato basam vacce super ollam posui."

9. [B 4]   (1) Salomon: "Nunc istud dimittamus, sed si in hac nocte non ita bene vigilaveris sicut ego, in crastino de capite tuo non poteris confidere." (2) Salomon et Marcolphus consederunt, parvoque intervallo facto Marcolphus dormire cepit et ructare. (3) Cui Salomon ait:"Dormis, Marcolphe?" Marcolphus respondit: "Non dormio, sed penso." (4) Salomon: "Quid pensas?" Marcolphus: "Penso tot in lepore esse juncturas in cauda quot in spina." (5) Salomon: "Nisi hoc probaveris, reus mortis eris." (6) Iterum, Salomone tacente, Marcolphus dormire cepit. Cui Salomon: "Dormis, Marcolphe?" Marcolphus: "Non dormio, sed penso." (7) Salomon: "Quid pensas?" Marcolphus: "Penso tot pennas albas in pica quot nigras." (8) Salomon: "Nisi etiam hoc probaveris, reus eris mortis." (9) Iterum, Salomone tacente, Marcolphus ructare et dormire cepit. Cui Salomon: "Dormis, Marcolphe?" Marcolphus: "Non dormio, sed penso." (10) Salomon: "Quid pensas?" Marcolphus: "Penso nullam rem sub celo esse candidiorem die."

8. (1) To that sayd Salomon alle laughyngly: "My folkys wayte upon me withoute. (2) I may no lengyr wyth thee talke, but saye to thy modyr that she sende me of hir beste cowe a pot full of mylke, (3) and that the pot of the same cowe be coveryd, and bringe thou it to me." (4) Marcolphus: "It shal be done." (5) King Salomon wyth his companye rydyng towardys Jerusalem was honourably receyvyd as a riche and moost puyssant king. (6) And whan Floscemya, Marcolphus modyr, was comyn home to hir house, he dede to hir the kinges message. (7) Than she, taking a pot full wyth mylke of hir cowe, and coveryd it wyth a flawne of the same mylke made, (8) and sent it so forth to the king by hir sone. (9) As Marcolphus went ovyr the felde, the wethir was warme of the sonne, sawe lying there a drye bakyn cowe torde, (10) and for haste he unnethe cowde set downe the pot to the erthe but that he had etyn the flawne and toke up the cowe torde and therwyth covyrd the pot, (11) and so covyrd presentyd it before the king. (12) And he askyd: "Why is the pot thus covyrd?" (13) Marcolf: "My lord, have not ye commaunded that the milke shulde be covyrd of the same cowe?" (14) Salomon: "I commaunded not so to be done." (15) Marcolph: "Thus I undyrstode." (16) Salomon: "It had ben bettyr coveryd wyth a flawne made wyth the mylke of the same cowe." (17) Marcolph: "So was it furste done, but hungyr chaungyd wyt." (18) Salomon: "How?" (19) Marcolph: "I wyste wele that ye had no nede of mete, and I havyng great hungyr ete the flawne wyth mylke anoynted, (20) and for that wyth wyt chungyd, the pot I have thus coveryd wyth a cowe torde."

9. (1) Salomon: "Now leve we alle this, and yf that thou thys nyght wake not as wele as I, thou mayste have no truste tomorne of thy hede." (2) Salomon and Marcolph consentyd bothe, and wythin a lytyll whyle aftyr Marcolph began to rowte. (3) Salomon sayde: "Marcolf, thou slepyst?" Marcolph answeryd: "Lord, I do not. I thinke." (4) Salomon: "What thinkyst thou?" Marcolf: "I thinke that there are as many joyntys in the tayle of an hare as in hire chyne." (5) Salomon: "If thou prove not that tomorne, thou arte worthy to deye." (6) Salomon beyng stylle, began Marcolph to slepe ayen, and sayde to hym: "Thou slepyst?" And he answeryd: "I do not, for I thynke." (7) Salomon: "What thynkest thou?" Marcolphus: "I thynke that the pye hath as many whyte fethrys as blacke." (8) Salomon: "But thou also prove that trewe, thou shalt lese thyn hede." (9) As Salomon ayen began to be stylle, Marcolph began ayen to rowte and to blowe, and Salomon sayd to hym: "Thou slepyst?" Marcolphus: "Nay, I thinke." (10) Salomon: "What thinkest thou?" Marcolph: "I thinke that undre th'erthe is no clerer thing than the daye."

8.1 **withoute,** outside. 8.3 **of the same cowe be coveryd,** be covered [by a product] of the same cow. 8.5 **puyssant,** powerful. 8.6 **dede to hir,** gave to her. 8.7 **flawne,** flan. 8.9 **drye bakyn cowe torde,** dry baked cow turd. 8.10 **unnethe cowde,** scarcely could. 8.16 **flawne,** flan. 8.17 **hungyr chaungyd wyt,** hunger changed [my] strategem (enhanced [my] cleverness). 8.19 **wyste wele,** knew well; **mete,** food; **the flawne wyth mylke anoynted,** the flan glazed with milk. 8.20 **wyth wyt chungyd,** substituted by wit (cleverness). 9.1 **wake,** stay awake; **no truste tomorne of thy hede,** no expectation in the morning of [retaining] your head. 9.2 **rowte,** snore. 9.4 **joyntys,** joints; **chyne,** chine (backbone). 9.7 **pye,** magpie. 9.8 **But,** Unless. 9.9 **rowte,** snore; **blowe,** breathe heavily. 9.10 **th'erthe,** the earth; **clerer,** clearer (i.e., brighter).

(11) Salomon: "Nunquid ergo dies candidior est lacte?" Marcolphus: "Est."
Salomon: "Probandum est hoc." (12) Post hoc Salomone tacente et vigilante
Marcolphus dormire et sufflare cepit. (13) Cui Salomon: "Marcolphe, adhuc
dormis?" Marcolphus: "Non dormio, sed penso." (14) Salomon: "Quid pensas?"
Marcolphus: "Nihil tute esse credendum mulieri." Salomon: "Et hoc a te
probabitur." (15) Iterum, Salomone tacente, Marcolphus sufflare et dormire
cepit. Cui Salomon: "Iterum dormis?" Marcolphus: "Non dormio, sed penso."
(16) Salomon: "Quid pensas?" Marcolphus: "Penso plus valere naturam quam
nutrituram." Salomon: "Nisi hoc probaveris, cras morieris." (17) Post hoc,
transacta nocte, Salomon fessus vigilando, se in loco suo collocavit.

10. [B 5]   (1) Tunc Marcolphus, dimisso rege, festinus cucurrit ad sororem suam,
Fudasam nomine, et similans se multum esse tristem, dixit ad eam: (2) "Rex
Salomon contrarius est mihi, et non possum pati minas et injurias ejus, sed ego
accipio cultellum unum sub veste mea, (3) et hodie, nesciente eo, infigam in cor
ejus et sic occidam eum. (4) Nunc autem, chara soror, precor te, ne me accuses,
sed omni fide zeles, nec etiam fratri meo Bufrido indices istud." (5) Cui Fudasa
respondit: "Chare frater Marcholphe, nihil dubites, (6) quia pro capite
perdendo non te accusarem." (7) Post hoc Marcolphus caute rediit ad curiam
regis.

11. [B 6]   (1) Sole autem terram illuminante, curia regis impletur, et Salomon a lecto
consurgens sedit in throno pallacii sui. (2) Tunc jussu regis lepus queritur, et
in sua presentia defertur, et tot juncture in cauda quot in spina a Marcolpho
numerantur. (3) Deinde quesita pica et coram rege illata, tot penne albe quot
nigre a Marcolpho numerantur. (4) Tunc rege nesciente Marcolphus lagenam
plenam lacte in cubiculo obstruxit ne lux intraret, (5) regemque vocavit.
Cumque rex intrare voluisset cubiculum, posuit pedem super lagenam plenam
lacte, et lapsus corruisset, nisi manibus se tenuisset. (6) Tunc rex iratus dixit:
"Tu fili perditionis, quid est quod fecisti?" (7) Marcolphus: "Irasci ab hac re
noli. Nonne dixisti quod lac esset candidius die? Quare non vidisti de lacte,
sicut de die vidisses? Equum judica! Nihil tibi peccavi." (8) Salomon: "Deus tibi
parcat! Vestis mea est perfusa, collum debuissem habere confractum de tuo
opere, et nihil mihi peccasti?" (9) Marcolphus: "Alia vice custodi te. Sed nunc
sedens fac mihi justiciam de proclamatione qua loquor ad te."

(11) Salomon: "Is the daye clerer than mylke?" Marcolph: "Ye." Salomon: "That muste thou prove." (12) Anone herupon began Marcolphus to slepe. (13) Salomon: "Thou slepyst." Marcolph: "I slepe not, but I muse." (14) Salomon: "What musyst thou?" Marcolph: "I muse how that men may not surely truste the women." Salomon: "And that of thee shal be provyd." (15) Anon aftyr as Salomon was stylle, began Marcolf ayen to blowe and to slepe. Salomon: "Thou slepyst?" Marcolph: "I do not, but I thinke." (16) Salomon: "What thinkest thou?" Marcolph: "I thinke how that nature goth afore lernyng." Salomon: "If thou prove not that trewe, thou shalt lese thyn hede." (17) Aftyr that the nyght was ovyrpassyd and Salomon, wery of waking, put hymself to reste.

10.   (1) Than Marcolf lefte the king and ran hastely to hys sustyr Fudasa and fayned hymself sorwefull and hevy, and sayde to hyre: (2) "The king Salomon is ayenst me, and I may not bere hys threytys and injuries, and but I shall take this knyf and hyde it secretly undyr my clothes, (3) and therewyth thys daye all pryvely, he not knowyng, I shall smyte hym to th'erte and sle hym. (4) Now good dere sustyr, I praye thee, accuse me not but in any wyse kepe it secrete, ne shewe it not to myn owne brothyr Bufrydo." (5) Fudasa answeryd: "My dere and leevest brothyr Marcolf, put no doubtes therin. (6) I had levyr dye and be brent at a stake rather than I shulde discovre it or accuse thee." (7) Aftyr that retournyd Marcolf alle pryvely towardys the kynges courte.

11.   (1) The sonne rysyng and spredyng hyr beamys ovyr th'erthe illumined and fulfyllyd the kingys palayce, and Salamon, rysyng from his bed, wente and sat in the trone or sete of his palayce. (2) Than commaunded he to bringe afore hym an hare, and as many joyntes in his tayle as in hys chyne were fownden by Marcolph and nombredyd. (3) Thanne was there a pye brought before the king, and as many whyte fethrys as black were fownden by Marcolph. (4) And thanne toke Marcolph a great panne wyth mylke and set it in the kinges bedchambre alle pryvely, and closyd to alle the wyndowes that no lyght myght in come. (5) Thanne kallyd he the king into the chambre, and as he come in he stumblyd at the panne and was nygh fallyn therin. (6) Tho was the king angry and displeasyd and sayd: "Thou fowle evyl body, what is it that thou doost?" (7) Marcolphus answeryd: "Ye ought not herefore to be angry. For have ye not sayd that milke is clerer than the daye? How is it that ye se not as wele by the clerenesse of the mylke as ye do bi the clerenesse of the daye? Juge egaly and ye shall fynde that I have nothyng mysdone unto you." (8) Salomon: "God foryeve thee! My clothys be alle wyth mylke sprongyn, and nygh I had my necke brokyn and yet thou haste me nothing trespasyd?" (9) Marcolphus answeryd: "Anothre tyme se bettyr tofore you. Nevyrthelesse, sytte downe and do me justyce upon a mater that I shall shewe afore you."

9.15 Anon aftyr as, As soon as; **blowe,** breathe heavily. **9.16 goth afore lernyng**; overrides upbringing or training. **10.1 fayned hymself;** pretended to be; **hevy,** sad. **10.2 threytys,** threats. **10.3 pryvely,** secretly; **th'erte,** the heart. **10.4 shewe,** reveal. **10.5 leevest,** most beloved. **10.6 had levyr dye,** would prefer to die; **discovre,** reveal. **10.7 pryvely,** secretly. **11.2 chyne,** chine (backbone); **nombredyd,** counted. **11.3 pye,** magpie. **11.6 Tho,** Then. **11.7 herefore,** on this account; **Juge egaly,** Judge impartially. **11.8 sprongyn,** sprayed. **11.9 tofore,** in front of.

12. [B 7]   (1) Cumque rex consedisset, Marcolphus conquerebatur dicens: "Habeo, domine, unam sororem Fudasam nomine, que meretrix effecta, que etiam pregnans dehonestat omnem parentelam meam, et tamen vult habere hereditatem paternam." (2) Tunc Salomon ait: "Vocetur ante nos soror tua et audiamus quid ipsa velit dicere." (3) Cunque fuisset vocata Fudasa coram rege, subridens rex Salomon ait: "Bene potest ista esse soror Marcolphi!" (4) Figura autem Fudase curta erat et grossa et impregnata, que ventre grossior erat, (5) et habuit spissas tibias, claudicansque utroque pede, vultu et oculis staturam Marcolpho similem gerens. (6) Rex Salomon ait ad Marcolphum: "Dic, quid conquereris de tua sorore." (7) Ad hoc Marcolphus consurgens dixit: "Domine rex, proclamationem facio coram te de sorore mea, que meretrix est effecta et pregnans, sicut videre potes, dehonestat omnem parentelam meam, (8) ac insuper vult habere partem hereditatis mee. (9) Quamobrem precor ut jubeas ne ipsa accipiat partem in ipsa hereditate." (10) Audiens hec Fudasa, repleta furore, prorupit in hanc vocem et dixit: "Pessime leccator, quare non haberem partem in hereditate mea? (11) Nonne, Marcolphe, genuit me Floscemia, que fuit mea mater, sicut et tua?" (12) Marcolphus: "Non habebis hereditatem, quia mediante tua culpa damnabitur tibi hereditas." (13) Fudasa ad hoc ait: "Non damnabitur mihi hereditas, quia, si peccavi, emendabo, sed juro per deum et per virtutes ejus, (14) nisi me dimiseris in pace, dicam talem rem, pro qua rex te suspensione faciet perire." (15) Marcolphus: "Sordida meretrix, quid dicere posses? Nil peccavi cuiquam." (16) Fudasa ait: "Multum peccasti, tu vilis nequam, (17) quia vis occidere dominum regem, et si non credatur mihi, queratur cultellus sub veste tua." (18) Cumque cultellus a familia quereretur et non inveniretur, (19) Marcolphus ait astantibus et regi: "Nonne verum dixi nil tute esse credendum mulieri?" (20) Cunque omnes elevassent risum, dixit Salomon: "Per ingenium omnia facis, Marcolphe." (21) Marcolphus: "Non est ingenium, sed quod credidi sorori mee, fraudulenter publicavit, sicut fuisset de veritate."

12.   (1) Whan he was set, Marcolph complayned and shewyd: "Lord, I have a sustyr that hath to name Fudasa, and she hath yeven hyrself to horedam and is wyth childe wherwyth she shamyth and dishonestyd alle oure bloode and lynage, and yet wolde she parte wyth me in my fathres good and herytage." (2) Thanne sayde Salomon: "Lete hyr come afore us, and we shall here hyr what she woll saye herto." (3) As Salomon sawe hyr come from ferre, sayde all laughyngly: "Thys may wele be Marcolphus sustyr!" (4) This Fudasa was short and thycke, and therto was she great with chylde, and thus was she thycker than she was of lenghthe. (5) She had thycke leggys and short, and went on fote lame, wyth vysage, yen, and stature lycke to Marcolph. (6) Salomon sayde to Marcolph: "What complaynest or askyst thou of thy sustyr?" (7) Marcolph answeryd: "My lord, I complayne and shewe opynly afore you of my sustyr, that she is a stronge harlot and a strumpet and is wyth chylde, as ye may se, and alle oure blood and kynrede by hyr is shamyd. (8) That wythstandyng, she wolde dele and parte wyth me in my fathres good and herytage. (9) Wherefore, I requyre you of justyce and that ye commaunde hire that she take no parte ne make no clayme therto." (10) This heryng, Fudasa, replete wyth angre and woednesse, cryed on hygh and sayde: "Thou fowle mysshapyn harlot, wherefore shulde not I have my parte in oure fadres good and herytage? (11) And is not Floscemya moder to us bothe?" (12) Marcolph: "Thou shalt not have any dele or parte therin, for thin offense jugeth thee clerely therfro." (13) Fudasa: "Therfore, I may not lese myn herytage. For have I mysdone, I shalle amende it, but oon thyng I promyse thee and swere by God and all hys myght. (14) Yf thou wylt not lete me be in pease and suffre me to have my parte in the land, I shall shewe suche a thyng of thee that the king, or it be nyght, shall do thee to be hangyd." (15) Marcolphus: "Thou fowle stynkyng hore, what kanst thou saye of me? I have no man mysdone. Saye thy worste, I dyffye thee." (16) Fudasa: "Thou haste moche misdone, thou fowle facyd knave and rybaulde that thou art. (17) For thou gladly woldyst sle the king, and yf ye beleve not me, seke undyr his cote and ye shall fynde the knyf." (18) Tho was the knyf sought by the kinges servauntys and it was not fownde. (19) Sayde Marcolph to the king and to the aboutestanders: "And have I not sayde trouthe, that men shulde not put ovyrmoche truste or confidence in the women?" (20) Wyth that they alle began to laughen. Tho sayd Salomon: "Marcolph, thou doost alle thy thynges by crafte and subtyltye." (21) Marcolph answeryd: "Lord, it is no subtyltye, but that my sustyr had promysed me to have kept it secrete, and she hath falsely discoverd it, as though it had ben of a trouthe."

12.1 shewyd, stated; **hath to name,** is named; **yeven hyrself to horedam,** given herself to whoredom; **dishonestyd,** dishonored; **lynage,** lineage (ancestry); **parte,** share; **my fathres good and herytage,** my father's goods and inheritable property. **12.3 ferre,** afar. **12.5 vysage,** face; **yen,** eyes. **12.8 That wythstandyng,** Nevertheless; **dele and parte,** divide up and share. **12.10 replete wyth angre and woednesse,** full of anger and fury; **harlot,** rascal. **12.12 dele,** portion; **jugeth thee clerely therfro,** clearly disqualifies you [from inheriting]. **12.14 suffre me,** allow me; **shewe,** reveal; **or,** before; **do,** cause. **12.15 dyffye,** defy. **12.16 fowle facyd knave and rybaulde,** foul-faced rascal and scoundrel. **12.21 discoverd,** revealed.

(22) Salomon: "Et quare dixisti plus valere naturam quam nutrituram?" (23) Marcolphus: "Sustine paululum, et antequam dormias ostendam tibi."

13. [B 8]   (1) Die autem transeunte et hora cene adveniente, rex sedit ad cenam cum maximo apparatu suorum, et Marcolphus sedens cum aliis inclusit tres mures in manicam tunice sue. (2) Fuerat enim in curia regis Salomonis cattus ita nutritus, ut omni nocte rege cenante teneret candelam duobus pedibus coram universis cenantibus stans, et duobus pedibus lucernam tenens. (3) Cum jam bene omnes cenassent, Marcolphus emisit unum de muribus, quem cum cattus respexisset et post illum ire voluisset, nutu regis est retentus. (4) Dumque de secundo mure factum fuisset similiter, Marcolphus emisit murem tercium, quem cum cattus conspexisset, ultra non tenens candelam, sed eandem rejecit, et post murem currens illum apprehendit. (5) Hoc Marcolphus videns dixit ad regem: "Ecce, rex, coram te probavi plus valere naturam quam nutrituram." (6) Dixit autem Salomon: "Projicite eum de conspectu meo. Si amplius venerit, dimittite super eum canes meos." (7) Marcolphus: "Nunc pro certo scio et dicere possum, quia ibi est mala curia, ubi non est justicia." (8) Cunque expulsus fuisset Marcolphus, cepit intra se dicere: "Neque sic neque sic sapiens Salomon de Marcolpho britone pacem habebit."

14. [B 9]   (1) Insequenti autem die de lectulo consurgens cogitavit quomodo curiam regis intrare posset, sic ut canes regis eum non devorarent. (2) Et abiens emit unum vivum leporem et posuit sub veste sua, sicque reversus est ad curiam regis. (3) Quem cum servi Salomonis vidissent, canes super eum ejecerunt. Marcolphus vero leporem emisit. Protinus canes Marcolphum relinquentes leporem invaserunt, et sic Marcolphus venit ad regem. (4) Cunque rex vidisset eum, dixit: "Quis te huc intromisit?" (5) Marcolphus respondit: "Calliditas non parva."

15. [B 10]   (1) Salomon: "Cave ne hodie mittas salivam de ore tuo nisi super terram." (2) Pallacium autem erat stratum tapetis, et parietes erant cooperti cortinis. (3) Cumque Marcolphus nimiam tussim haberet, et inter colloquia ejus saliva nimia in ore ejus habundaret, respiciens circa se vidit hominem calvum juxta regem stantem. (4) Tunc in angustia grandi positus, cum non videret nudam terram, super quam screare posset, collegit salivam in ore cum magno impetu, et screavit in frontem calvi hominis. (5) Mox calvus iste nimio rubore perfusus frontem suam detersit et se ad pedes regis prostravit, et proclamationem de Marcolpho fecit.

(22) Salomon: "Wherefore haste thou sayd that arte or nature goth before lernyng?" (23) Marcolph: "Take pacyence a lytyll, and afore or ye go to bedde, I shal shewe you."

13. (1) The daye passyd ovyr and the tyme of souper cam on. The king sat to sowper and othre wyth whom sat Marcolph and had alle pryvely put into hys sleve thre quyk myse. (2) There was norysshyd in the kinges house a catte, that every nyght as the king sat at sowper was wont to holde betwyxt hyre forefeet a brennyng kandell upon the tabyll. (3) Thanne lete Marcolph oon of the myse go out of his sleve. As the catte that saugh, she wolde have lept aftyr, but the king yave hyr a wynke or countenaunce that she bode stylle syttyng and removyd not. (4) And in lyke wyse dede she of the secunde mowse. Thanne lete Marcolph the thrydde mowse go, and as the katte sawe she cowde no lenger abyde, but kaste the kandell awaye, and lept aftyr the mowse and toke it. (5) And as Marcolph that sawe, sayde to the king: "Here I have now provyd before you that nature goth afore lernyng." (6) Tho commaunded Salomon his servauntes: "Have thys man out of my syghte, and if he come hythre any more, set my howndes upon hym." (7) Marcolphus: "Now for certayne I knowe and may saye that where as the hede is seke and evyll at ease, there is no lawe." (8) As Marcolph was thus out dryven, he seyde to hymself: "Neythre so nor so shall the wyse Salomon of Marcolf be quyte."

14. (1) On the next mornyng folowyng as he was out of his couche or kenel rysen, he bethoughte hym in his mynde how he myght beste gete hym ayen into the kinges courte wythout hurte or devouryng of the howndes. (2) He went and bought a quyk hare and put it undre his clothis, and yede ayen to the courte. (3) And whan the kinges servauntes had syghte of hym, they set upon hym alle the howndes, and forthwyth he caste the hare from hym, and the howndes aftre, and lefte Marcolph, and thus came he ayen be the king. (4) And as he sawe hym, he askyd who had letyn hym in. (5) Marcolph answeryd: "Wyth great sutyltie am I in comen."

15. (1) Salomon: "Beware that thys daye thou spytte not but upon the bare grownde." (2) The palayce was all coveryd wyth tapettys, and the walles hangyd wyth riche clothys. (3) Marcolf wythin short space aftyr wyth his talkyng and clateryng wyth othre, his mouth was full of spytyll, began to cough and reche up, (4) beholdyng al aboute hym where he myght best spytte and cowd fynde no bare erthe, sawe a ballyd man stondyng by the king barehedyd, and spatyld evyn upon his forehede. (5) The ballyd man was therwyth ashamyd, made clene his forehede, and fyll on kneyes before the kingys fete, and made a complaynt upon Marcolph.

12.22 Wherefore, Why; **goth before lernyng,** overrides training. **12.23 afore or,** before. **13.1 pryvely,** secretly; **quyk myse,** live mice. **13.2 wont,** accustomed; **brennyng kandell,** burning candle. **13.3 yave,** gave; **countenaunce,** facial expression; **bode stylle syttyng,** remained still. **13.4 dede she of,** did she in response to; **abyde,** stay still. **13.5 goth afore lernyng,** overrides upbringing or training. **13.7 seke,** sick; **evyll at ease,** ill at ease. **13.8 of Marcolf be quyte,** be rid of Marcolf. **14.1 kenel,** kennel; **ayen,** again. **14.2 quyk,** live; **yede ayen,** went again. **14.3 forthwyth,** immediately; **ayen be,** again by. **15.2 tapettys,** carpets. **15.3 clateryng,** chattering; **spytyll,** spittle; **reche up,** retch. **15.4 ballyd,** bald; **spatyld,** spat.

(6) Salomon: "Quare fedasti frontem calvi hujus?" (7) Marcolphus: "Non fedavi, sed fimavi. In sterili enim terra fimus ponitur, ut segetes in ea abundantius multiplicentur." (8) Salomon: "Et hoc quid pertinet ad calvum hominem?" (9) Marcolphus: "Nonne prohibuisti ut hodie non screarem nisi super terram nudam? Vidi enim frontem nudam capillis et credens esse nudam terram ideo screavi in eam. (10) Non irasci debet rex pro hac re, quia pro suo proficuo feci. Si frons ejus frequenter sic fuisset rigata, capilli reverterentur." (11) Salomon: "Deus te confundat! Nam calvi homines sunt ceteris honestiores, quia calvitium enim non est vicium, sed honoris initium." (12) Marcolphus: "Calvicium est magis muscarum ludibrium. Non conspiceo, rex, quomodo musce insequuntur frontem illius calvi magis quam ceterorum frontes capillorum? (13) Putant namque esse aliquod vas tornatile pleno aliquo bono potu aut esse aliquem lapidem delinitum aliqua dulcedine, et ideo infestant nudam frontem ejus." (14) Ad hec coram rege calvus ait: "Ut quid vilissimus nequam intromittitur ante regem nos vituperare? Eiciatur foras!" (15) Marcolphus: "Et fiat pax in virtute tua, et tacebo!"

16. [B 11]   (1) Interea venerunt due mulieres ferentes unum vivum puerum, de quo coram rege contendebant. (2) Nam una dixit: "Meus est infans." Altera: "Non, sed meus est." Sed una earum dormiens suum oppresserat filium, unde coram Salomone pro vivo puero contendebant. Nam una dixit: "Meus est," etc. (3) Ad hoc Salomon dixit servis: "Afferte gladium et dividite infantem, et unaqueque mulier accipiat partem infantis." (4) Quod audiens mulier cujus vivebat filius ad regem dixit: "Obsecro, domine, date illi infantem vivum. Hec est enim mater ejus."

17. [B 12]   (1) Marcolphus querit a rege: "Quomodo nosti hanc esse matrem pueri?" (2) Salomon: "Ex affectione et mutatione vultus et effusione lachrimarum." (3) Marcolphus: "Non bene. An credis lacrimis femine? Tu sapiens nescis artes mulierum? (4) Dum femina plorat oculis, corde ridet; plorat uno oculo, ridet altero; (5) ostendit vultu quod non habet affectu; loquitur ore quod non cogitat mente; (6) hoc sepe promittit quod implere non cupit; sed immutatur vultus, per varia ejus ingenia cursitat cogitatus.

(6) Salomon: "Wherefore haste thou made fowle the forehede of this man?" (7) Marcolph: "I have not made it fowle, but I have dungyd it or made it fat. For on a bareyne grownde, it behovyth dunge to be layde, that the corne that is theron sowyn may the bettyr growe and multiplye." (8) Salomon: "What is that to this man?" (9) Marcolph: "My lord, have ye not forbedyn me that this daye I shulde not spytte but upon the bare erthe? And I sawe his forehede alle bare of herys, and thynkyng it be bare erthe, and therefore I spyttyd upon it. (10) The king shall not be angry for this thing for I have done it for the manys proffyte, for and if his forehede were thus usyd to be made fat, the herys shulde ayen encrease and multiplye." (11) Salomon: "God yeve thee shame! For the ballyd men aught to be aboven othre men in honure, for balydnesse is no shame, but a begynnyng of worshipe. (12) Marcolphus: "Balydnesse is a flyes nest. Beholde I not, syre, how the flyes folowe more his forehede than alle the othre that ben wythin thys house? (13) Forwhy they trowen that it be a vessell turnyng full wyth som good drinke or ellys to be a stone anoynted wyth any swete thyng, and therfor they haste thaym to his bare forehede." (14) To this sayd the ballyd man afore the king: "Wherto is this moost vyle rybaulde sufferyd in the kinges presence us to rebuke and shame? Lete hym be kast out!" (15) Marcolph: "And be it pease in thy vertu, and I shal be stylle."

16.   (1) Herewythall come yn two women bryngyng wyth thaym a lyving chylde, for the wyche they afore the king began to stryve. (2) For the oon sayde it belongyd to hyre, but the oon of thaym had forlayne hyre chylde slepyng so that they were in stryve for the levyng chylde. (3) Salomon sayd to oon of his servauntis: "Take a sworde and departe thys chylde in two pecys, and yeve eyther of thaym the oon half." (4) That heryng, the naturall modyr of the lyvyng chylde sayde to the king: "Lord, I beseche you, yeve it to that woman all hool lyvyng for she his the verraye modyr therof." Than sayde Salomon that she was the modyr of the chylde and yave it to hire.

17.   (1) Marcolph demaunded of the king how he the modyr knewe. (2) Salomon: "By chaungyng of hir colure and affection, and by effusyon of terys." (3) Marcolphus: "Ye myghthe so be disceyved, for beleve ye the wepyng of the women, and are so wyse and knowe the crafte of thaym no bettyr? (4) Whyllys a woman wepyth, she laughyth wyth th'erte. They kan wepe wyth oon yie and lawgh wyth the othyr. (5) They make contenaunce wyth the vysage that they thinke not. They speke wyth the tunge that they mene not wyth th'erte. (6) They promyse

---

15.7 made it fat, fertilized it; **bareyne,** barren; **it behovyth dunge to be layde,** it is necessary to spread dung; **corne,** grain. **15.10 the manys proffyte,** the man's benefit. **15.13 Forwhy they trowen,** Because they believe; **turnyng,** returning. **15.14 Wherto,** Why; **rybaulde,** scoundrel. **15.15 be it pease in thy vertu,** Let peace be in thy strength. **16.1 stryve,** quarrel or struggle. **16.2 forlayne hyre chylde slepyng,** suffocated her child by lying on it while asleep; **levyng,** living. **16.3 departe . . . in two pecys,** divide in two pieces; **yeve eyther of thaym,** give each of them. **16.4 all hool lyvyng,** whole and alive; **his the verraye modyr therof,** is the [child's] true mother. **17.2 effusyon of terys,** flow of tears. **17.4 Whyllys,** While; **th'erte,** the heart; **oon yie,** one eye. **17.5 make countenaunce wyth the vysage,** express emotions with the face.

(7) Innumeras artes habet femina." (8) Salomon: "Quot habet artes, tot habet probitates." (9) Marcolphus: "Non dic probitates, sed pravitates et deceptiones." (10) Salomon: "Vere illa fuit meretrix, que talem genuit filium." Marcolphus: "Cur hoc dicis, domine rex?" (11) Salomon: "Quia tu vituperas muliebrem sexum. Est enim mulier honesta, concupiscibilis, honorabilis et amabilis." (12) Marcolphus: "Adhuc potes adiungere quod sit fragilis et flexibilis." (13) Salomon: "Si est fragilis, per humanam conditionem talis est, si flexibilis, per delectationem talis est. (14) Mulier enim de costa hominis est facta, et homini in bonum adjutorium et delectamentum data. (15) Nam mulier potest dici quasi mollis res." (16) Marcolphus: "Similiter mulier potest dici quasi mollis error." (17) Salomon: "Mentiris, nequam pessime. Pessimus enim esse potes, omnia mala loquens de muliere. (18) De muliere enim nascitur omnis homo, et qui ergo dehonestat muliebrem sexum, nimium est vituperandus. (19) Unde quid divicie, quid regna, quid possessiones, quid aurum, quid argentum, quid preciose vestes, quid preciosi lapides, quid sumptuosa convivia, quid leta tempora, quid delicie valent sine femina? (20) Vere potest vocari mundo mortuus, qui est ab hoc sexu segregatus. (21) Femina enim generat filios et filias, nutrit et diligit eos, amplectitur, optat salutem eorum. (22) Femina regit domum, sollicita est pro salute mariti et familie. (23) Femina est delectatio rerum omnium, femina est dulcedo juvenum, femina est consolatio senum, exhilaratio puerorum. (24) Femina est gaudium diei, solacium noctis, laborum alleviatio, omnium rerum tristium oblivio. (25) Femina servit sine dolo, servetque introitus et exitus meos." (26) Ad hoc Marcolphus ait: "Verum dicit, qui dixit: 'Quod in corde, hoc est in ore.' (27) Multum amas feminas et ideo laudas eas. Divicie, nobilitas, pulchritudo et sapientia concordant tibi, et ideo amores tibi concordant mulierum. (28) Sed dico tibi quam nunc laudas eas, et antequam tu dormias vituperabis eas." (29) Cui Salomon: "Mentiris, quia omnibus diebus vite mee mulieres amavi, amo et amabo. (30) Sed nunc discede a me et vide ne amplius in conspectu meo male loquaris de muliere."

18. [13]   (1) Tunc Marcolphus pallacium regis exiens vocavit ad se meretricem illam, cui restitutus fuit filius vivus, et dixit ad illam: "Scis quid actum sit in curia regis?"

many tymes that they parforme not, but they chaunge theyre contenaunces as theyre myndes renne. (7) The women have innumerable craftes." (8) Salomon: "As many craftes as they have, so many good condicyons and propyrtyes they have." (9) Marcolphus: "Saye not good condicyons or propyrtyes, but saye shrewdnessys and decepcyons." (10) Salomon: "Surely she was an hore that bare suche a sone." Marcolph: "Wherefore saye ye so?" (11) Salomon: "For thou blamyst alle women, and they are honest, chaste, meke, lovyng, and curtayse." (12) Marcolf: "To that myght ye adde and saye that they are brotyll and mutable." (13) Salomon: "If they be brotyll, that have they of manys condicyon; yf they be chaungeable, that have they by delectacioun. (14) Woman is though made of mannys rybbe and yeven unto hym for his helpe and comfort. (15) For *woman* is as moche to saye as a 'weyke erthe' or a 'weyke thynge.'" (16) Marcolph: "In like wyse it is as moche to saye as a 'softe erroure.'" (17) Salomon: "There lyest thou, false kaytyf. Thou muste nedys be evyll and onhappy that sayst so moche shame and harme of women. (18) For of women we are alle comen, and therfore he that seyth evylle of the kynde of women is greatly to be blamyd. (19) For what is rychesse, wat is kingdomes, what is possessions, what is goold, what is sylver, what is costely clothyng or preciouse stonys, what is costely metys or drinkes, what is good companye or solace, what is myrthe withoute women? (20) On trouthe, they may kalle wele the world deed that from women are exiled or banysshed. (21) For women muste bere the chyldren, they fede and norysshe thaym up, and love thaym welle. She desyryth thayre helthys. (22) She governyth the household. She forwyth the helthe of hyr husband and household. (23) Women is the dilectacioun of alle thinges. She is the swetnesse of youthe. She is the solace or joye of age. She is gladnesse of childre. (24) She is joye of the daye. She is solace of the nyght. She is the glad ynd of laboure. Of alle hevynesses she is the forgeter. (25) She servyth withhoute grutchyng, and she shall watche my goyng out, and myn incomyng." (26) Therupon answeryd Marcolphus: "He seyth trouthe that thinkyth wyth his herte as he spekyth wyth his mowth. (27) Ye have the women in great favoure, and therfore ye prayse thaym. Rychesse, nobylnesse, fayrenesse, and wysedom be in you, and therfore it behovyth you to love women. (28) But Y assure you one thyng, albeit that ye now prayse thaym ovyr moche, or ye slepe ye shal dysprayse thaym as faste." (29) Salomon: "Therof thou shalt lye, for alle my lyve dayes I have lovyd women and shall duryng my lyf. (30) But now go from me and se wele to that before me thou nevyr speke evyll of women."

18.   (1) Than Marcolphus, goyng out of the kynges palayce, kallyd to hym the woman that had hir childe to hyre yeven ayen by the king and sayd to hyre: "Knowyst thou not what is done and concluded in the kingys counsell todaye?"

17.6 as theyre myndes renne, i.e., as they choose. **17.8 condicyons,** qualities. **17.9 shrewdnessys,** wickednesses. **17.10 Wherefore,** Why. **17.12 brotyll,** morally weak (untrustworthy). **17.13 manys condicyon,** the human condition; **by delectacioun,** as a delightful thing. **17.14 yeven,** given. **17.15 woman,** i.e., the word *woman,* L *mulier* (see explanatory note). **17.17 kaytyf,** wretch. **17.20 may kalle wele,** may well call; **deed,** dead; **that from women,** that from which women. **17.22 forwyth,** aids. **17.23 dilectacioun,** source of pleasure. **17.24 ynd,** end; **hevynesses,** sorrows. **17.25 grutchyng,** complaining. **17.28 albeit that,** even though; **or,** before. **18.1 yeven ayen,** returned.

(2) At illa respondit: "Filius meus mihi concessus est vivus, sed quid factum sit prorsus ignoro." (3) Cui Marcolphus: "Rex precepit ut crastina die tu voceris et socia tua, et dabitur tibi media pars filii tui, et illi altera similiter." (4) Ad hoc mulier ait: "O quam malus rex et quam male et inique sententie ejus!" (5) Tunc Marcolphus dixit: "Adhuc graviora dicam tibi et deteriora. (6) Nam rex et consiliarii sui statuerunt ut unusquisque vir accipiat septem uxores. Unde pensa quid de eis faciendum sit. (7) Quia si unus vir septem habuerit uxores, nunquam erit domus in pace. (8) Una namque amabitur, altera despicietur. Quia illa que magis viro placuerit, cum marito frequentius erit, que vero minus placuerit, cum marito rarius erit. (9) Una ergo bene vestietur, altera nuda relinquetur. Dilecta habebit anulos, monilia, argentum, et aurum, varium et sericum. (10) Custodiet claves domus, honorabitur a familia, et vocabitur domina. Omnes divicie mariti cedunt ei. (11) Cumque sic una amabitur, quid alie sex dicture sunt? Si due, quid alie quinque? Si quatuor, quid alie tres? Si quinque, quid alie due? Si sex, quid una? (12) Tunc osculabitur, amplexabitur et marito sociabitur. (13) Que videntes, [quid] dicture sunt aut referant? Nec enim vidue nec maritate, nec cum marito nec sine marito erunt. Penitebit enim eas perdidisse virginitatem. (14) Ire, rixe, contentiones, emulationes et invidie inter eas semper erunt, perpetuum odium inter eas regnabit, et nisi prohibitum fuerit hoc malum, una preparabit alteri venenum. (15) Quamobrem, quia femina es et nosti muliebrem sexum, festina nunciare dominabus omnibus quibus potes hujus civitatis, et dic eis ut omnino non consentiant, sed contradicant regi et consiliariis ejus."

19. [B 14]   (1) Cunque Marcolphus caute rediisset ad curiam regis Salomonis et consedisset in angulo pallacii, (2) illa meretrix, credens verba ejus esse vera, transvolans per medium urbis et palmas suas pectusque suum quatiens, verba que audierat undique divulgabat. (3) Et sic concursus matronarum fiebat, vicina referebat vicine, et oriebatur ingens tumultus mulierum. Et sub parva hora quasi omnes femine seu mulieres totius urbis in unum congregebantur. (4) Quibus congregatis placuit eis consilium, et agmine facto magno, iverunt ad pallacium regis Salomonis. Venientes itaque ad curiam regis Salomonis quasi septem milia mulierum vallaverunt pallacium sive aulam regis Salomonis, et impetu facto fregerunt valvas ejus, et convicia horrenda ei inferebant et consiliariis ejus. Una vero plus, altera minus, omnes simul coram rege voces emittebant.

20. [B 15]   (1) Tandem rex, vix imperato silentio, requisivit quenam esset causa tanti tumultus. Ad hoc una que inter omnes constantior et eloquentior ceteris videbatur, dixit ad regem: (2) "Tu rex, cui aurum et argentum et lapides preciosi omnesque divicie terrarum deferuntur, facis omnes voluntates tuas et nullus voluntatibus tuis resistit.

(2) She answeryd: "My chylde is yevyn me ayen alyve, what ellys there is done, that knowe not I." (3) Tho sayd Marcolph: "The king hath commaunded and is uttyrly determyned that tomorwe thou and thy felawe shall come ayen afore hym, and that thou shalt have the one half of thy chylde and thy felawe the othre half." (4) Than sayde the woman: "O what evyll king, and what false and untrewe sentence yevyth he!" (5) Marcolph sayde: "Yet shall I shewe thee grettyr matiers and more chargeable, and of grettyr weyghte. (6) The king and his counseyle hath ordeyned that evyr man shall have vii wyves, therfor remembre and thinke what therin is best to be done. (7) For as one man hath vii wyves, so shall ther nevyr more be reste or pease in th'ouse. (8) One shal be belovyd, anothre shall displease hym. For hir that he lovyth shal be moost wyth hym, and the othre nevyr or seldom. (9) She shal be wele clothyd, and the othre shal be forgetyn. Hyr that he lovyth best shall have ryngys, jowellys, goold, sylvyr, furres, and were sylkys. (10) She shal kepe the keyes of alle the house, she shal be honouryd of alle the servauntys and be kallyd 'Mastres.' Alle his goodes shall falle to hire. (11) What shall than saye the othre vi? And yf he love tweyne, what shall the othre v saye? And yf he love thre, what shal saye the othre iiii? and yf he love iiii what shall the othre iii do, etc.? (12) That he lovyth best, he shall alwayes have by hym and kysse hire and halse hyre. (13) The othyr shall nowe saye that they are neythre wydowes nor weddyd, nor yit unweddyd, nor wythoute husbande. They shal nowe well forthynke that they have theyre maydenhede loste. (14) There shall evyr stryff, angre, envye, and brawelyng reigne, and if there be not fownde a remedy herefore, many great inconvenyencys shall growe thereof. (15) And by cause that thou arte a woman, and well acqueynted wyth the condicyons of women, haste thee and shewe thys to alle the ladyes and women wythin this citie, and advyse thaym that they consente not to it in any wyse, but wythstande it and saye ayenst the king and his counseyll."

19.   (1) Marcolf retourned and went ayen to the courte and pryvely hyd hym in a corner. (2) And the woman trowyd his wordys to be trewe, ranne trough the citie, and clappyd hire handys togydre, and cryed wyth opyn mowthe and shewyd all that she had herd and more. (3) And eche neyghborwe or gossyp saide it forth to anothre, so that in short tyme there was a great assemble or gaderyng of women, wel nigh that alle the women that weren wythin the citie, (4) and so gadred, went to the kynges palayse well by the nombre of vi thousand women, and brak up dorys and ovyrwent the kyng and his counsell wyth great malyce and lowde crying.

20.   (1) The king, as he this herde, axyd what the cause was of thayre gaderyng. To that, oon woman that wyser and more eloquent than the othre sayde unto the king: (2) "Moost myghty prynce to whom goold, sylver, preciouse stones, and alle

---

18.2 **yevyn me ayen alyve,** returned to me alive; **ellys,** else. 18.3 **Tho,** Then. 18.5 **chargeable,** serious. 18.7 **th'ouse,** the house. 18.9 **were,** wear. 18.10 **'Mastres,'** 'Mistress' (as a term of respect). 18.11 **tweyne,** two of them. 18.12 **halse,** embrace. 18.13 **forthynke,** regret. 18.15 **wythstande,** resist; **saye ayenst,** speak against. 19.1 **ayen,** again; **pryvely,** secretly. 19.2 **trowyd,** believed; **shewyd,** revealed. 19.4 **ovyrwent,** overcame. 20.1 **axyd,** asked.

(3) Habes reginam et reginas plures, super hoc inducis concubinas innumerabiles quot vis. Es unicuique quantum vis, quia habes omne id quicquid vis. (4) Hec facere omnes non possunt." (5) Salomon respondit: "Unxit me deus in regem in Israhel, et non potero exequi voluntates meas?" (6) Ad hec mulier inquit: "Satis fac voluntatibus tuis de tuis, de nobis cur faceres? Nos nobiles de genere Abrahe sumus et legem Moysi tenemus. (7) Quare vis immutare legem nostram? Qui debes facere justiciam, cur facis injusticiam?" (8) Ad hoc Salomon furore repletus ait: "Quam exerceo injusticiam, pudibunda mulier?" (9) Mulier ait: "Maxima injusticia est quia vis constituere, quod unusquisque mas septem uxores accipiat. Certe non fiet istud. (10) Non est dux neque comes neque princeps, qui sit tantarum diviciarum seu potentiarum, qui uni soli uxori suas impleat voluntates. (11) Quid faciet, si septem uxores habuerit? Supra vires hominum est istud facere. Melius est enim ut unaqueque habeat septem viros." (12) Ad hec Salomon rex subridens dixit suis: "Non estimabam numerum hominum posse equari multitudine mulierum." (13) Tunc omnes mulieres Jherosolimitane una voce clamaverunt: "Vere malus rex es tu et injuste sentencie tue. (14) Nunc vero scimus quia vera sunt que audivimus. Malum tractas de nobis, et derides nos coram nobis. (15) O deus! quam hora mala prius Saul regnavit super nos, quam pejus David, quam pessime iste Salomon regnavit!"

21. [B 16]   (1) Tunc rex in iram prorumpens dixit: "Non est caput nequius super caput colubri, et non est ira super iram mulieris. Commorari leoni et draconi magis placebit quam habitare cum muliere nequam. (2) Brevis est omnis malicia et minor super maliciam mulieris. (3) Sors peccatorum cadit super eam, sicut ascensus arenosus in pedibus veterum, sicque mulier linguosa mulierisque ira et irreverentia confusio magna est. (4) Mulier si primatum habet, contraria est viro suo. (5) Cor humile, facies tristis et plaga mortis mulier nequam est. (6) Mulier enim initium est peccati et per illam omnes morimur. Dolor cordis et luctus mulier zelotipa. In muliere infideli flagellum lingue omnibus communicans. (7) Fornicatio mulierum in excellentia oculorum et in palpebris illius agnoscetur. Ab omni reverentia oculi ejus sunt, et ne mireris, si te neglexerint."

22. [B 17]   (1) Talia rege referente Nathan propheta assurgens dixit: "Cur dominus meus rex confundit facies omnium Jherosolomitarum mulierum?" (2) Salomon: "Nonne audisti quanta vituperia sine mea culpa mihi injecerunt?"

rychesse of the world to you are brought, ye do alle thyng as ye woll, and non ayensayth youre pleasure. (3) Ye have a quene and many quenys, and ovyr that ye have concubynes or paramours wythoute nombre or as many as you pleasyth, for ye have all that ye wol. (4) So may not every man do." (5) Salomon answeryd: "God hath anoynted and made me king in Israhel. May I not than do and accomplyssh all my wylle?" (6) She answeryd: "Do youre wylle wyth youre owne, and medle not wyth us. We are of the noble blood of Abraham and holde Moyses lawe. (7) Wherfor woll ye thane that chaunge and altre? Ye are bownden to do right and justyce. Wherefore do ye unryght?" (8) Tho sayde Salomon wyth great unpacyence: "Thou shamfull wyf, what unright or wronge do Y?" (9) She answeryd: "As great unright do ye as kan be thought or ymagined. For ye have ordeyned that every man shal have nowe lawefully vii wyves, and certaynli that shall not be. (10) For there is not that prynce, duke, or erle that so riche and puyssaunt is, but that oon woman alone shall now fullfylle alle his desyres and wylle. (11) What thanne shulde he do wyth vii wyves? It is aboven any mannys myght or power. It were bettyr ordeyned that oon woman shulde have vii husbondes." (12) Than sayd Salomon all laughyngly: "I had not trowed that of men had ben fewer in nombre than of women." (13) Tho kryed alle the women as mad people wythoute any reason: "Ye are an evyle king and youre sentences ben false and unrightfull. (14) Now may we wel here and se that it is trouthe that we have herd of you, and that ye have of us sayde evyll, and therto ye skorne and mocke us before oure vysages that we se it. (15) O Lord God, who was so evyle as Saule that regnyd ovyr us furste? Yet Davyd was worse, and now this Salomon werst of alle!"

21.   (1) Than the king beyng full of wrathe sayde: "There is no hede more worse than the serpent, and there is no malyce to the malyce of a woman, for it were bettyr to dwelle wyth serpentys and lyons, than wyth a wyckyd woman. (2) Alle evylles are but lytyl to the cursydnesse of a shrewd woman. (3) Alle wyckydnesse falle upon women as the sande fallyth in the shoes of the oolde people goyng up an hylle. So a talkatyf woman and dishobedyent is a great confusyon. (4) That wyf that is hir husbondes maister is evyr contrarye to hym. (5) An evyl wyf makyth a pacient herte, and a sory vysage and is as plage of the deth. (6) A woman was the begynnyng of synne, and through hire we dye alle. (7) The woman that is luxuriouse may men knowen in the uppermest of hire yes, and by hir browes. For hire yes are wythoute revyrence and ther nede no man wondre although she forgete hir husbonde."

22.   (1) As the king al thus had sayd, so spak Nathan the prophete and sayde: "My lord, why rebuke ye and shame ye thus alle thies women of Jherusalem?" (2) Salomon: "Have ye not herd what dishonoure they have sayd of me wythoute

---

20.2 **ayensayth,** speaks against. **20.3 paramours,** lovers; **wol,** desire. **20.6 Moyses,** Moses'. **20.7 Wherfor; Wherefore,** Why. **20.10 puyssaunt,** powerful. **20.12 trowed,** believed. **20.13 Tho,** Then; **sentences,** judgments or words of wisdom; **ben,** are. **20.14 vysages,** faces. **21.1 hede,** head. **21.2 shrewd,** wicked. **21.5 sory vysage,** sorrowful face; **plage,** plague. **21.7 luxuriouse,** lustful; **yes,** eyes.

(3) Continuo Nathan respondit: "Cecus, surdus et mutus ad tempus debet esse, qui in pace cum subjectis esse desiderat." (4) Salomon respondit: "Respondendum est stulto secundum suam stulticiam." (5) Tunc saliens Marcolphus de loco suo in quo sedebat dixit ad regem: "Bene loquutus es voluntatem meam, Salomon. Quoniam heri laudasti feminas multum, modo vituperas eas. (6) Hoc ego volebam, semper enim me facis veracem." (7) Salomon: "Quid est hoc, furcifer? Numquid cognosti tumultum istum?" (8) Marcolphus: "Non ego, sed pusillanimitates earum. Non debes credere quicquid audieris." (9) Tunc rex ait: "Discede a me, et cave ne amplius videam te in mediis oculis." (10) Confestim Marcolphus ejectus est de pallacio regis.

23. [B 18]   (1) Illi autem, qui regi astabant, dixerunt: "Loquatur dominus noster rex in auribus mulierum istarum ut dimittantur." (2) Tunc rex conversus dixit mulieribus: "Sciat dulcedo vestra me innocentem esse coram vobis, et sine culpa esse de oppositis. Ille callidus leccator, quem modo vidistis, hec omnia confinxit. (3) Unusquisque vir uxorem suam habeat, et illam cum fide et honestate diligat. (4) Quid vero dixi de muliere, nisi de muliere nequam dixi? De bona muliere quis diceret mala? (5) Pars enim bona mulier bona. (6) Gratia mulieris sedule delectabit suum virum et ossa illius inpinguabit disciplina illius. (7) Datum est dei. Mulier sensata et tacita gratia super omnem gratiam. (8) Mulier pudica sicut sol oriens in altissimis dei. Sic mulieris bone species est ornamentum domus sue. (9) Lucerna splendens super candelabrum et species super etatem stabilem. (10) Columne auree super bases argenteas et pedes firmi super plantas, stabilis mulieris fundamentum eternum super petram solidam, et mandata dei in corde mulieris. (11) Sanctus dominus deus Israhel ipse benedicat vos, et multiplicet semen vestrum in generationibus seculorum." (12) Cunque respondissent omnes 'Amen', adorato rege, recesserunt.

24. [B 19]   (1) Marcolphus vero moleste ferens injuriam sibi de rege factam, et quod jusserat ut eum amplius in mediis oculis non videret, cogitabat quid ageret. (2) Deinde, nocte insequuta, nix multa de celo in terram cecidit. (3) Tunc Marcolphus cepit cribrum unum in manu una, et pedem ursi in manu altera, et calciamenta sua transversa, et quasi bestia quatuor pedibus per plateas urbis cepit ire.

deservyng?" (3) Nathan answeryd: "He that woll wyth hys subgiettys lyve in reste and pease, he muste som tyme be blynde, dumme, and deef." (4) Salomon: "It is to be answeryd to a fole aftyr his folysshnes." (5) Tho sprange Marcolph out of the corner that he sat in and sayde to the king: "Now have ye spokyn aftyr myn intent. For ones thys daye ye praysed women out of alle mesure, and now have ye dispraysed thaym as moche. (6) That is it that I sought, alwayes ye make my saying trewe." (7) Salomon: "Thou fowle evyle body, knowyst thou of this commocion?" (8) Marcolph: "Nay. Nevyrthelesse, ye shulde not yeve credence to alle thing that ye here." (9) Tho sayd the king Salomon: "Go from hens out of my syghte, and I charge thee that I se thee no more betwixt the yes." (10) Forthwith was Marcolph kast out of the kinges palayse.

23. (1) Thanne they that stoden by the king sayden: "My lord, speke to thiese women sumwhat that may please thaym to here to th'entent that they may departe." (2) Than turnyd the king towardes thaym and sayd: "Youre goodnesse shal undrestande that I am not to be blamyd in that that ye laye to my charge. That evyl sayer, Marcolf, that ye here late sawe, hath out of hymself alle this matier surmysed and fayned. (3) And every man shall have hys owne wyf and hyr, wyth faythe and honestie, love and cherysshe. (4) That I have spokyn ayenst the wyves, I have not sayde it but ayenst the froward wyves. Who shulde of the good wyves speke any evyll? (5) For a good wyf makyth hyr husbande glad and blythe wyth hyre goodnesse. (6) She is a parte the lyvyng of hyre husbond upon erthe, and hyr lernyng advauntagyth or forthryth hys body. (7) She is a yifte of God. A wyse wyf and a stylle is a grace aboven graces. (8) A good, shamefast and an honeste wyf is lyke the sonne clymmyng up to God. A wyf of good condicyons is the ornament or apparayle of the house. (9) She is a lyght shynyng bryghther than the lyght of candellys. (10) She is lyke the goolden pyller standyng upon hir feet, and an ovyrfaste fundament grwnded upon a sure stone wythoute mutacions and the commandemantys of God evyr in hyr mynde. (11) The Hooly God of Israhel blesse you and multiplye youre sede and kynderede unto the ende of the worlde." (12) Tho sayde they alle 'Amen' and toke leve of the king and went theyre weyes.

24. (1) Marcolph, beryng in his mynde of the unkyndnesse that the king had commanded hym that he shulde no more se hym betwixt the yes, thought in hymself what was best to do. (2) It happenyd that the next nyght folowyng fyll a great snowe. (3) Marcolphus toke a lytyll cyve or temse in his oon hande, and a foot of a bere in the othre hande, and he turnyd hys shoes that stode forwardes upon his feet bakward, and upon the mornyng erly he began to go lyke a beste

---

22.3 subgiettys, subjects. **22.5 Tho,** Then; **out of alle mesure,** without moderation. **22.8 yeve credence to,** believe. **22.9 hens,** hence; **se,** see; **betwixt the yes,** between the eyes. **22.10 Forthwith,** Directly. **23.1 here,** hear; **to th'entent that,** so that. **23.2 that ye laye to my charge,** of which you accuse me; **surmysed,** alleged; **fayned,** invented. **23.4 but,** except; **froward,** evil. **23.6 a parte the lyvyng,** an allotted portion in life; **forthryth,** aids. **23.7 stylle,** quiet, peaceable. **23.8 shamefast,** modest (virtuous); **clymmyng,** climbing; **condicyons,** qualities. **23.10 ovyrfaste fundament,** strong foundation; **grwnded,** grounded. **23.11 sede and kynderede,** seed and kindred. **24.1 se hym betwixt the yes,** see him between the eyes. **24.2 fyll,** fell. **24.3 cyve,** sieve; **temse,** strainer; **bere,** bear.

(4) Cum autem venisset extra civitatem invenit furnum unum, et intravit in eum. (5) Nocte autem abeunte, dies venit, et familiares regis surgentes tramitem Marcolphi invenerunt, et estimantes esse tramitem alicujus mirabilis bestie, regi nunciaverunt. (6) Tunc rex cum copula canum, et cum venatoribus suis, cepit prosequi vestigia Marcolphi. Cum autem venissent ante furnum et vestigia defecissent, (7) descendunt ad os furni inspicere. (8) Marcolphus vero latebat in facie sua curvatus, et deposuit bracam suam apparebantque ei nates, et culus, et curgulio, et testiculi. (9) Que videns rex ait:"Quis est qui ibi jacet?" (10) "Marcolphus ego sum," respondit. (11) Salomon: "Quomodo," inquit, "ita jaces?" (12) Marcolphus: "Tu precepisti mihi, ne amplius me videres in mediis oculis. Nunc autem si non vis me videre in mediis oculis, videas me in medio culi."

25. [B 20]   (1) Ad hoc rex Salomon confusus ait servis: "Apprehendite et suspendite eum in ligno." (2) Apprehensus autem Marcolphus dixit ad regem: "Domine mi rex, tantummodo mihi impendere potes, ut in illo ligno quod elegero, suspendar." (3) Salomon rex ait: "Fiat quod petisti, mihi enim pro minimo est in quo suspendaris ligno." (4) Tunc ministri regis Marcolphum capientes, duxerunt extra civitatem et pertranseuntes vallem Josaphat, et clivum Montis Oliveti pervenerunt usque Jhericho, et nullam arborem invenire potuerunt, quam Marcolphus suo suspendio eligeret. (5) Inde transeuntes Jordanem, et peragentes omnem Arabiam, et iterum nullam arborem Marcolphus elegit. Inde circumeuntes saltum Carmeli, et cedros Libani, et solitudinem campestrium circa Mare Rubrum, (6) et nunquam Marcolphus aliquam arborem elegit. (7) Et sic evasit manus regis Salomonis. Post hoc domum remeans quievit in pace.

Finitum est hoc opusculum Antwerpie
per me Gerardum Leeu

upon alle fowre feet through the strete. (4) And whan he was comen a lytyll wythouthe the towne, he fownde an olde ovyn and crept into it. (5) And as the lyght of the daye was on comen, oon of the kingys servauntys founde the footstappys of Marcolph and thougt that it was the trace or stappys of a merveylous beste, and in alle haste went and shewyd it to the king. (6) Thanne incontynent wyth huntres and howndes, he wente to hunte and seke the sayd wondrefull beeste and folowed it unto they comen before the oven where they had loste and fownde no more of the steppys. (7) The king Salomon discended from hys hors and began to loke into the oven. (8) Marcolphus laye all crokyd, hys vysage from hymwardes, had put downe hys breche into hys hammes that he myght se hys arshole and alle hys othre fowle gere. (9) As the kyng Salomon, that seyng, demawnded what laye there, (10) Marcolph answeryd: "I am here." (11) Salomon: "Wherefore lyest thou thus?" (12) Marcolf: "For ye have commaunded me that ye shulde no more se me betwyxt myn yes. Now and ye woll not se me betwyxt myn yes, ye may se me betwene my buttockys in the myddes of myn arsehole."

25. (1) Than was the king sore meovyd, commaunded his servauntys to take hym and hange hym upon a tre. (2) Marcolph, so takyn, sayde to the kyng: "My lord, will it please you to yeve me leve to chose the tre wherupon that I shalle hange?" (3) Salomon sayde: "Be it as thou haste desyred, for it forcyth not on what tre that thou be hangyd." (4) Than the kinges servauntes token and leddyn Marcolph wythoute the citie, and through the Valé of Josaphath, and ovyr the hyghte of the hylle of Olyvete, from thens to Jericho and cowde fynde no tre that Marcolf wolde chese to be hanged on. (5) From thens went they ovyr the Flome Jordane and alle Arabye through, and so forth all the great wyldernesse unto the Rede See. (6) And nevyrmore cowde Marcolph fynde a tre that he wolde chese to hange on. (7) And thus he askapyd out of the dawnger and handes of King Salomon, and turnyd ayen unto hys howse, and levyd in pease and joye. (8) And so mote we alle do aboven wyth the Fadre of Heven. Amen.

Emprentyd at Andewerpe by me M. Gerard Leeu.

24.5 trace, trail; **stappys,** [foot]steps. **24.6 incontynent,** immediately. **24.8 hys vysage from hymwardes,** facing away from him; **breche,** britches; **hammes,** hams (thighs or backs of the knees); **se,** see; **gere,** gear (equipment). **24.11 Wherefore,** Why. **24.12 yes,** eyes; **and,** if. **25.1 sore meovyd,** annoyed (distressed). **25.2 yeve me leve,** give me permission. **25.3 it forcyth not,** it does not matter. **25.4 wythoute,** outside; **Valé of Josaphath,** Valley of Jehoshaphat; **hylle of Olyvete,** Mount of Olives. **25.5 Flome Jordane,** River Jordan. **25.7 askapyd,** escaped.

Figure 5. *Solutions to Riddles Posed by Marcolf to Solomon.* From *Frag und Antwort Salomonis und Marcolfi.* Nuremburg: M. Ayrer, 1487. Reproduced by permission of the Bibliothèque nationale de France, Paris. Shelfmark: BN Rés. Y2 884, fol. avj.

 **EXPLANATORY NOTES**

ABBREVIATIONS: **B**: *Salomon et Marcolfus*, ed. Benary; **CT**: Chaucer, *Canterbury Tales*; **L**: Latin; **ME**: Middle English; **MED**: *Middle English Dictionary*; **Whiting**: Whiting, *Proverbs, Sentences, and Proverbial Phrases*.

	Here begynneth. The ME translation includes an incipit or opening summary based on the description of Marcolf in the opening passages of the work proper. Its language may also derive from the lengthy *Collationes* title (see introduction 6.c). Leeu's Latin edition bears the title *Salomonis et Marcolphi Dyalogus*.
1.1	*Salomon . . . sate*. [B Prol.] 3 Kings 2:12, "And Solomon sat upon the throne of his father David" ["Salomon autem sedit super thronum David patris sui"]. Compare 3 Kings 2:24 and 1 Paralipomenon (1 Chronicles) 29:23.
2.1–3.6	*short stature and thykke*. [B Prol.] Coarse, animal-like features are conventional in medieval descriptions of peasants (Freedman, *Images of the Medieval Peasant,* chap. 7). The language applied to Marcolf and his wife can be compared, for example, to Chaucer's description of his stoutly built ("thikke") and hairy Miller (*CT* I[A]545–66, at 549). Marcolf has a beard like a goat's, the Miller like that of a sow or fox. Marcolf's hair also resembles a goat's, his face that of an ass. Polycana has eyebrows like the "brostelys of a swyne" (3.2); the Miller's wart has sprouting hairs like "the brustles of a sowes erys [ears]." The Miller and Polycana have large, flaring noses, the Miller's with "nosethirles blake . . . and wyde" and Polycana's with "right great nosethrylles" (3.5).
2.3	L *subcominus*. [B Prol.] The word is unattested; many manuscripts have *subterius* [lower].
2.3	*fowle*. [B Prol.] The ME translator reads *fetosam* [foul]; the Leeu Latin print has *setosam* [hairy, bristly.] The confusion of *f* and *s* is common in fifteenth-century manucripts and prints.
2.6	*his clothys fowle and dyrty*. [B Prol.] L *pellis* [hide; peasant's cloak]; *pannitiosus* [tattered, ragged.]
2.7	*his hasyn hynge full of wrynkelys*. [B Prol.] In classical Latin, *caligae* are soldiers' boots, but the plural here seems to mean "stockings, hose." Ziolkowski (*Solomon and Marcolf,* p. 113) suggests "patched and repatched" for L *repagulatus*.
3.3	*vysage and skyn*. [B Prol.] In Leeu's Latin print (3.2), Polycana has an "aspectum colubrinum" [face like a snake]. The ME translation omits this comparison.

3.7   *thies verses folowyng.* [B Prol.] The two elegiac couplets are clear in their
           misogyny but obscure in meaning. Literally, they mean, "The ill-shapen
           woman, subjected to the forms of darkness, / With her ugly face passes by
           without the light of day. / It is a bad thing to grant excessive adornment to an
           ugly woman, / But let the ugly woman endure her very ugly defect." Leeu's
           Latin print has *transit* [passes by (or through)]; some manuscripts have
           transeat [let her pass by], which offers better sense. The ME translator does
           not translate the two couplets, preferring to supply the gist of their meaning.
           His language is identical to a Dutch translation of 1501, indicating that the
           two translations are related (see introduction, 6.c).

3.8   *wyf.* [B Prol.] ME *wyf* translates L *femina* and often means simply "woman."

4.1a–3b   *of what lynage . . . xii kyndredes of patryarkes . . . xii kindred of chorlys . . . xii
           kyndredes of untydy wyves.* [B 1a–3b] We follow Benary in numbering this
           section as part of the proverb contest, although we regard the exchange of
           genealogies as a separate verbal contest. Solomon's words at 4.3a suggest
           that it has served as a kind of preliminary match, qualifying Marcolf for the
           next round, a long exchange of what are usually called "proverbs" for conve-
           nience, though they include various types of remarks.

4.2a   *Ysay.* [B 2a] Solomon's genealogy makes Isai David's father, as at Ruth
           4:17–22; the more familiar genealogies at Matthew 1:1–6 and Luke 3:32
           make Jesse his father.

4.2b   *Rusticus gat Rustam.* [B 2b] Marcolf improvises a parodic genealogy that
           includes derivatives from *rusticus* [peasant, country person] and forms of his
           own name. *Tarcus* may derive from *tartarum* [wine dregs] and *Pharsi* could
           derive from *far*, a type of grain. See Marini, *Il dialogo di Salomone e Marcolfo*,
           p. 140n8; Ziolkowski, *Solomon and Marcolf,* pp. 116–17.

           Marquat gat Marcolphum and that is I. In the Latin text, Solomon's genealogy
           ends with the declaration *et ego sum Salomon rex* [and I am Solomon the king].
           Marcolf ends with the parallel declaration *et ego sum Marcolphus follus* [and I
           am Marcolf the fool]. Interestingly, the ME translator, both here and at 6.1,
           omits *follus* [fool], an epithet that resonates with Marcolf's many twists on the
           biblical and proverbial idea that the self-styled "wise man" is in reality the
           fool, and the self-aware "fool" is the wiser man. See for example 4.6ab,
           4.16ab, 4.51ab, 4.64ab, 4.79ab, and esp. 7.1–10, as well as these exchanges
           in the appendix: B 89ab, B 90ab, B 115ab.

4.2c   *untydy wyves.* [B 2c] The ME translator's softening of *lupicanae* [whores] from
           lupa [she-wolf].

4.3a   *altercacion.* [B 3a] (The ME text reads *altercacon.*) A formal academic debate.
           Woodcuts accompanying printed versions of the *Dialogue* often show the two
           speakers using their hands to count off debating points, a conventional way
           of representing academic disputation (Jones, "Marcolf the Trickster," p. 152).
           Over the course of the work, the two interlocutors alternate in the roles of
           master (who initiates and questions) and pupil (who must respond appropri-

ately). Solomon first requires that Marcolf recite his genealogy and then declares that Marcolf must "answere" him (4.3a) in the proverb contest. At 6.3–4 Marcolf usurps the role of master or wisdom figure and initiates a third verbal contest, posing riddles that Solomon cannot solve. Solomon then retakes the initiative by posing the "covered by the same cow" riddle at 8.2–3. Solomon also initiates the waking contest at 9.1 by threatening to decapitate Marcolf if he falls asleep, but Marcolf introduces the five propositions for which Solomon then demands proof. Finally, Marcolf initiates the last major verbal contest by implying at 17.28 that he can lead Solomon into self-contradiction by causing him to dispraise women as strongly as he praised them at 17.18–25.

questyons to thee. Echoing God to Job at Job 38:3, "I will ask thee, and answer thou me" ["interrogabo te, et responde mihi"]; see also Job 40:2 and 42:4.

4.3b   *He that singyth worste*. [B 3b] Samuel Singer (*Sprichwörter*, 1:53) gives analogues for the equivalent Latin expression, "Qui male cantat, primo incipiat."

4.4a–4.91b   The proverb contest. In this long exchange, Marcolf's responses in Latin include a number of close verbal parodies of Solomon's scripture-based pronouncements as they occur in the wisdom books of the Latin Vulgate Bible. Unlike the expressions we usually call proverbs, these made-for-the-occasion Marcolfian verbal parodies would not have circulated in common speech. They might better be called mock-proverbs, though many draw upon traditional ideas that do occur in proverbial form. In Leeu's Latin text, Marcolf's responses imitate closely the language of Solomon's proverbs in these exchanges: 4.13ab, 4.15ab, 4.71ab, 4.72ab, 4.79ab, 4.81–84ab. At least seventeen more exchanges of this type are present in the fullest manuscripts but do not appear in the printed texts: they are included in our appendix as numbered by Benary: B 15ab, B 26ab, B 30–34ab, B 38ab, B 40ab, B 46ab, B 48ab, B 69ab, B 89ab, B 112ab, B 125ab, B 128ab, and B 138ab. The exchanges omitted from the printed texts represent some of the most transgressive pairings, many involving scathing scatological parody of scriptural language, substituting "shit" for "wisdom," for example, or "the arse" for "the Lord."

While many of Marcolf's contributions involve close verbal parody of Solomon's biblical proverbs in Latin, others of Marcolf's replies are indeed recognizable proverbs that enjoyed wide circulation in the Middle Ages in Latin and often in the European vernacular languages as well. Translating Latin proverbs to and from the vernacular was a standard medieval school exercise, and a great many proverbs have migrated from one language to the other. (See Steiner, "Vernacular Proverb in Mediaeval Latin Prose," and, on medieval England, Orme, *Education and Society*, pp. 76–85.) Ziolkowski cites many parallels to the Latin proverbs; for the most part we concentrate here on identifying expressions attested in ME outside the *Dialogue*. Whiting includes most of Marcolf's responses in his index of English proverbs before 1500, but in many cases he is not able to cite any other example of the expression in question. We give Whiting numbers when his entry lists examples in English from outside the ME *Dialogue of Solomon and Marcolf* or provides cross-references, even if the attestation expresses the same idea in different words. We do not give the many Whiting numbers that simply lead the reader to Marcolf's expression with no other information.

4.5a   *juged betwixt two light women.* [B 5a] For Solomon's judgment, see 3 Kings 3:16–27.

4.5b   *where women be there are wordys.* [B 5b] Whiting W497 gives versions of an antifeminist proverb in English that is obviously related to Marcolf's: "There women are are many words, there geese are are many turds." Another related expression in English is W253, "A young wife and a harvest goose, much gaggle (chatter) with both."

4.6a   *God yave wysdam.* [B 6a] 3 Kings 3:11–13, "And the Lord said to Solomon: Behold I. . . have given thee a wise and understanding heart, insomuch that there hath been no one like thee before thee, nor shall arise after thee. . . . I have given thee. . . riches and glory, so that no one hath been like thee among the kings in all days heretofore" ["et dixit Dominus Salomoni. . . dedi tibi cor sapiens et intelligens in tantum ut nullus ante te similis tui fuerit nec post te surrecturus sit. . . dedi tibi divitias scilicet et gloriam ut nemo fuerit similis tui in regibus cunctis retro diebus"].

4.6b   *He that hath evyll neighborys praysyth hymself.* [B 6b] Singer, *Sprichwörter,* 1:50, Whiting N79; compare Whiting P349, "He must praise himself since no man else will."

4.7a   *wykkyd man fleyth.* [B 7a] Proverbs 28:1, "The wicked man fleeth, when no man pursueth" ["Fugit impius, nemine persequente"].

4.7b   *Whan the kydde rennyth, men may se his ars.* [B 7b] Whiting K22, with reference to a related expression about seeing the backside of a climbing ape. Marcolf's statement about the white markings of a fleeing deer or roebuck (L *capriolus*) has its basis in observation of nature. Solomon moralizes about the ill effects of a bad conscience; Marcolf's characteristic reply stresses the kinship between humans and animals and reminds Solomon of what Bakhtin calls "the material bodily lower stratum," the parts of the body associated with defecation and filth but also with fertility and birth.

4.8a   *good wyf.* [B 8a] Ecclesiasticus 26:21, "As the sun when it riseth to the world in the high places of God, so is the beauty of a good wife for the ornament of her house" ["Sicut sol oriens mundo in altissimis Dei, sic mulieris bonae species in ornamentum domus ejus"]; Proverbs 12:4, "A diligent woman is a crown to her husband" ["Mulier diligens corona est viro suo"].

4.8b   *potfull of mylke.* [B 8b] Whiting C109 cites a sixteenth-century expression about the irresistibility of milk to a cat. In 4.12b Marcolf poses a similar thought as a rhetorical question.

4.9a	*wyse woman byldeth.* [B 10a] Proverbs 14:1, "A wise woman buildeth her house: but the foolish will pull down with her hands that also which is built" ["Sapiens mulier aedificat domum suam; insipiens exstructam quoque manibus destruet"].
4.9b	*that clene is browyn.* [B 10b] Benary's edition has "olla bene cocta melius durat, et qui merdam distemperat merdam bibit" [A well-fired (earthenware) pot stands up very well to use, but whoever stirs in shit, drinks shit]. Leeu's Latin print substitutes the sense-destroying *mundam* [clean, fine] for *merdam* in the second clause. The ME text does not translate the apparently garbled second clause of the Latin text; rather, it offers a meaningful and logically consistent second clause, "what is brewed cleanly is good to drink." "To drink as one brews" is a ME proverbial expression that takes many forms (see Whiting B529; Singer, *Sprichwörter*, 1:35–36).
4.10a	*A ferdefull woman shal be praysed.* [B 11a] Proverbs 31:30, "the woman that feareth the Lord, she shall be praised" ["mulier timens Dominum ipsa laudabitur"].
4.10b	*A catte that hath a good skyn shal be flayne.* [B 11b] Another of many instances in which Marcolf responds to Solomon's sententious pronouncements about humanity with cynical statements about animals. Whiting C99 gives two examples of the related saying that a cat with a fair skin shows itself abroad while a singed cat stays home. The expression occurs in Chaucer's Wife of Bath's Prologue (*CT* III[D]348–54), where the fictional Wife implies that her misogynist husbands applied it to her. An application to women is also implied here by the juxtaposition of Marcolf's reply to Solomon's statement.
4.11b	*whyte mete.* [B 12b] L *lacticinia* [dairy products (?)], obviously from *lac* [milk], but the meaning is unclear. Benary's edition reads "vacca lactiva" [a cow producing milk], but *lactivus* occurs in no major dictionaries.
4.12a	*woman stronge in doyng good.* [B 13a] Proverbs 31:10, "Who shall find a valiant woman? far and from the uttermost coasts is the price of her" ["Mulierem fortem quis inveniet? procul et de ultimis finibus pretium ejus"].
4.13b	*A fat woman and a great is larger in yevyng than othre.* [B 14b] Leeu's Latin print says that the fat woman is larger or more generous [*largior*] in giving *visa* [things seen], which the translator apparently omits as nonsensical. Some manuscripts read *in dando jussa* [in giving farts], a reading which fits well with Marcolf's persistent scatology.
4.14b	*furre is not all lyke the slevys.* [B 16b] L *pellicia* [fur coat]. The idea that a fair exterior can hide ugliness or corruption is widespread proverbial wisdom; see Ziolkowski, *Solomon and Marcolf*, p. 129, for Latin examples. That a woman's attractive exterior hides ugliness or destructive qualities underneath is a commonplace of antifeminist discourse.
4.15ab	*He that sowyth wyckydnesse shal repe evyll.* [B 17ab] Proverbs 22:8, "He that soweth iniquity shall reap evils" ["Qui seminat iniquitatem metet mala"]. Compare Job 4:8; Galatians 6:8. The idea appears frequently in medieval

sermons and proverb collections; see Whiting S542 for instances in English. Solomon uses the image of sowing and reaping metaphorically to warn against wickedness; Marcolf's reply is more concrete and agricultural, especially in ME: "he who sows chaff [the lifeless outer husks that surround the fertile grain] mows a poor harvest."

4.16b   *The asse behovyth to be allweye where he fedyth.* [B 19b] The longest of Marcolf's retorts and one of the most revealing. The medieval association between peasants and asses (and other beasts of burden) was very strong. See Bakhtin, *Rabelais*, p. 78: "The ass is one of the most ancient and lasting symbols of the material bodily lower stratum, which at the same time degrades and regenerates"; see also Freedman, *Images of the Medieval Peasant*, pp. 48, 134, 140–47. Marcolf's statement that the ass's dung fertilizes the ground and his urine waters it implies a symbolic justification for the scatology and crudeness of his replies to Solomon: his fertilizing scatology helps to regenerate Solomon's static and aging discourse. Of the connection between defecation and fertility, Bakhtin writes, "To degrade . . . means to concern oneself with the lower stratum of the body, the life of the belly and the reproductive organs; it therefore relates to acts of defecation and copulation, conception, pregnancy, and birth. Degradation . . . has not only a destructive, negative aspect, but also a regenerating one" (*Rabelais*, p. 21). Marcolf returns to the connection between bodily emissions and fertility in 15.1–10.

    strawe. Leeu's Latin print, like most of the manuscripts, has *glebas* [clods of earth]. Breaking up the clods is a final example of the animal's positive effect on the soil of the field where it grazes. The point is somewhat obscured by the ME translation, *strawe*.

4.17a   *Lete an othre preyse thee.* [B 20a] Proverbs 27:2, "Let another praise thee, and not thy own mouth: a stranger, and not thy own lips" ["Laudet te alienus, et non os tuum; extraneus, et non labia tua"].

4.18a   *Thou shalt ete moche ony.* [B 23a] In Leeu's Latin print, the command is negative ["ne comedas"], a curtailed version of the biblical dictum at Proverbs 25:16, "Thou hast found honey, eat what is sufficient for thee, lest being glutted therewith thou vomit it up" ["Mel invenisti, comede quod sufficit tibi, ne forte satitus evomas illud"], and 25:27, "As it is not good for a man to eat much honey. . ." ["sicut qui mel multum comedit non est ei bonum"]. The ME text makes Solomon's prohibition into a positive commandment, and the mention of honey opens the way for another allusion to animal husbandry from Marcolf.

4.19a   *In an evylle wylled herte the spyryt of wysedome shalle not entre.* [B 24a] Wisdom 1:4, "For wisdom will not enter into a malicious soul" ["quoniam in malivolam animam non intrabit sapientia"].

4.19b   *As ye smyte wyth an axe in an hard tre, beware that the chippes falle not in youre ye.* [B 24b] Whiting C235. The proverb appears in ME in various forms, e.g., John Gower, *Confessio Amantis* 2.1917–18, "Fulofte he heweth up so hihe [high], / That chippes fallen in his yhe [eye]."

4.20a   *It is hard to spurne ayenst the sharp prykyl.* [B 25a] Acts 26:14 (Jesus to Saul of Tarsus), "It is hard for thee to kick against the goad" ["Durum est tibi contra stimulum calcitrare"]. A *prykyl* or goad is a spiked object, used as a spur to drive an animal. The expression warns against the futility and pain of running up against an intractable obstacle.

4.21a   *Fede up youre children and from thayre youthe lerne thaym to do welle.* [B 35a] Proverbs 19:18 and 29:17, "Erudi filium tuum" [chastise (or "instruct") your son].

4.22b   *A worne tabyllcloth turnyth ayen to his furste kynde.* [B 37b] Leeu's Latin literally says "A worn out tablecloth turns back into flax fiber / hemp." See Ziolkowski, *Solomon and Marcolf*, pp. 141–42, for commentary on a variant Latin text.

4.23a   *What the juge knowyth of right and trouthe that spekyth he out.* [B 39a] Compare Proverbs 12:17, "He that speaketh that which he knoweth, sheweth forth justice: but he that lieth, is a deceitful witness" ["Qui quod novit loquitur index justitiae est; qui autem mentitur testis est fraudulentus"].

4.23b   *bisshop that spekyth not.* [B 39b] Marcolf's response appears to comment wryly on the rarity of silence among bishops: a silent bishop would be out of a job as bishop.

4.24a   *Honoure is to be yeven to the maistre, and the rodde to be feryd.* [B 41a] Compare Proverbs 29:15, "The rod and reproof give wisdom: but the child that is left to his own will bringeth his mother to shame" ["Virga atque correptio tribuit sapientiam; puer autem qui dimittitur voluntati suae confundit matrem suam"].

4.24b   *juges handes. . . asse lene.* [B 41b] The man who bribes a judge ("greases his palm") has no money left to feed his pack animal. The Latin text refers to the judge's mouth [*buccam*], but the ME translator prefers "hands." L *azella, asella* is a "she-ass."

4.25a   *Ayenst a stronge and myghty man thou shalt not fyghte, ne stryve ayenst the streme.* [B 43a] Compare Ecclesiasticus 8:1, "Strive not with a powerful man, lest thou fall into his hands" ["Non litiges cum homine potente, ne forte incidas in manus illius"], and 4:32, "Resist not against the face of the mighty, and do not strive against the stream of the river" ["Noli resistere contra faciem potentis, nec coneris contra ictum fluvii"].

4.25b   *vultier takyth the skyn.* [B 43b] To Solomon's image of coercion as an impersonal force of nature such as a rushing stream, Marcolf responds with a harsh image of predation. Singer (*Sprichwörter*, 1:37) notes that the vernacular poet Marcabru uses a version of this expression.

4.27b   *wyt.* [B 45b] L *ingenium* or ME *wyt* is Marcolf's most salient quality in this dialogue; his improvisational cleverness is repeatedly matched against Solomon's *sapiencia* or moral wisdom. Here Marcolf's response implies that the clever man makes a point of greeting someone who is eating so that the eater is pressured to share. (The Latin text makes it clearer that "the other" is eating.) Incessant hunger is another of Marcolf's characteristic traits.

4.28a   *Wyth brawlyng people holde no companye.* [B 47a] Compare Proverbs 22:24, "Be not a friend to an angry man, and do not walk with a furious man" ["Noli esse amicus homini iracundo, neque ambules cum viro furioso"].

4.28b   *It is reson that he of the swyne ete that medlyth amonge the bren.* [B 47b] Leeu's Latin literally says "Rightly do the swine eat him who wanders into the bran." Ziolkowski (*Solomon and Marcolf*, p. 147) cites various Latin proverbs to this effect, with the implication that one must watch where one is going and whom one is with. In the Latin text, Marcolf's thought parallels Solomon's at 4.28a but transposes it into barnyard imagery. The ME translation reverses the thought and makes the man the eater of the swine; the reversal disrupts the parallel with Solomon's admonition.

4.30a   *There are many that to theyr good doers do evyl for good.* [B 50a] Compare Proverbs 17:13, "He that rendereth evil for good, evil shall not depart from his house" ["Qui reddit mala pro bonis, non recedet malum de domo ejus"].

4.31a   *It is no frende that dureyth not in frendeshyp.* [B 51a] Proverbs 17:17, "He that is a friend loveth at all times: and a brother is proved in distress" ["Omni tempore diligit qui amicus est; et frater in angustiis comprobatur"].

4.32a   *from his maister.* [B 52a] The Latin has *ab amico* [from a friend]. Proverbs 18:1, "He that hath a mind to depart from a friend seeketh occasions" ["Occasiones quaerit qui vult recedere ab amico"].

4.32b   *she hath a skabbyd arse.* [B 52b] The implication of this antifeminist proverb seems to be either that a woman will claim to have a scabby arse as an excuse for not having sex or, perhaps more in keeping with Marcolf's sense of humor as it emerges later in the work, he may be claiming (as a disincentive to refusal) that a woman who refuses to have sex is thereby admitting that her backside is scabby.

4.33b   *plowyth wyth a wolf.* [B 53b] Leeu's Latin text reads *lupo* [wolf], and the translator follows suit, but the best manuscripts read *vulpes* [fox], and the folly or impossibility of plowing with a fox was already proverbial in antiquity, as Ziolkowski demonstrates (*Solomon and Marcolf*, p. 150).

4.34ab *radissh rotys.* [B 54a] The exchange plays on the theme of eating radishes as a source of bad breath, burping, and farting.

4.35b   *in the sande.* [B 56b] The translator has tried to make sense of the obscure reading *trimpum / tripum*; Benary prints *scirpum* [rush, bulrush].

4.36a   *He that stoppyth his erys.* [B 57a] Compare Proverbs 21:13, "He that stoppeth his ear against the cry of the poor, shall also cry himself and shall not be heard" ["Qui obturat aurem suam ad clamorem pauperis, et ipse clamabit, et non exaudietur"].

4.37ab   *Ryse up, thou northren wynde...* [B 58ab] Solomon quotes from Canticles (Song of Songs) 4:16; Marcolf contradicts Solomon's positive image of the north wind by referring to its destructive potential. The contrast suggests that a north wind aroused more positive associations in the biblical Holy Land than it did in medieval Europe. Here the ME text translates only the first line of the two-line poem in the Latin text; the second line reads, "He who has a hernia is not in good health."

4.38b   *A man that is brostyn and hyde it, they growe the more.* [B 59b] References to digestion, defecation, and diseases, such as the scabby arse in 4.32b or the hernias here, are part of Marcolf's ongoing insistence on the needs, frailties, and indignities of the body.

4.39a   *As thou syttyst at a riche mans table, beholde diligently what comyth afore thee.* [B 63a] Proverbs 23:1, "When thou shalt sit to eat with a prince, consider diligently what is set before thy face" ["Quando sederis ut comedas cum principe, diligenter attende quae apposita sunt ante faciem tuam"].

4.40a   *Whan thou syttyst at the tabyll, beware that thou taste not furst.* [B 64a] Ecclesiasticus 31:12, "Art thou set at a great table? be not the first to open thy mouth upon it" ["Supra mensam magnam sedisti, non aperias super illam faucem tuam prior"].

4.41b   *The catte seeth wele whoos berde she lycke shall.* [B 65b] Whiting C108. This widespread proverb appears in ME in various forms, including this example from a bilingual collection of c. 1300: "Well wot hure [our] cat, whas berd he lickat" / "Murelegus bene scit, cuius barbam lambere suescit." It appears in Latin as well as in the Old French *Li Proverbe au vilain* and in the ME *Proverbs of Hending* (c. 1325); its meaning varies by context (Singer, *Sprichwörter*, 1:38–40). Here in the mouth of Marcolf it could reassert the power of the seemingly weaker but craftier member of a pairing: Solomon says that the strong man takes all from the weak; Marcolf's reply may mean that a cat knows very well how to get what it wants from a human.

4.42a   *That the wycked feryth, that fallyth hym often.* [B 67a] Proverbs 10:24, "That which the wicked feareth, shall come upon him" ["Quod timet impius veniet super eum"].

4.43a   *For the colde the slouthfull wolde not go to plough.* [B 68a] Proverbs 20:4, "Because of the cold the sluggard would not plough: he shall beg therefore in the summer, and it shall not be given him" ["Propter frigus piger arare noluit; mendicabit ergo aestate, et non dabitur illi"].

4.43b   *A nakyd ars no man kan robbe or dispoyle.* [B 68b] Solomon warns that the lazy man who does not plant his crops may not be able to beg bread when he is hungry; Marcolf's rejoinder suggests that a man with nothing has nothing to lose. Marcolf's expression is Whiting A196, with no other examples, but a related saying, B528, occurs in a sixteenth-century dialogue in proverbs by John Heywood, "There is nothyng more vayne . . . Than to beg a breeche of a bare arst man" (*A dialogue conteynyng the number of the effectuall prouerbes in the Englishe tounge*, in Heywood, *Works*, pp. 18–101).

4.45b   *An angry howsewyf.* [B 75b] A widespread proverb that goes back to scripture and thus might be thought to belong to Solomon's discursive world rather than Marcolf's: "a wrangling wife is like a roof continually dropping through" (Proverbs 19:13), "Roofs dripping through in a cold day, and a contentious woman are alike" (Proverbs 27:15). Proverbs 10:26 testifies to the irritation to the eyes caused by smoke. Medieval writers commonly refer to "three things" that cause a man to flee his own house (see Ziolkowski, *Solomon and Marcolf*, p. 162, for Latin examples; Whiting T187 for English versions). Often the "three things" are the elements from scripture: a scolding wife, a leaking roof, and smoke. Compare Chaucer's Wife of Bath's Prologue, *CT* III(D)278–80, and Tale of Melibee, *CT* VII(B²)1086; also William Langland, *Piers Plowman*, B.17.319–24, for a husband plagued by the same three, including, with Langland's characteristic concreteness, "reyne on his bedde." In Benary's manuscript-based edition, Marcolf gives just two irritants in the form of a short proverb poem: "Domina irata / et patella perforata / dampnum sunt in casa" [An angry woman and a pan with holes are ruinous in a house]. The Latin printed editions, including Leeu's, add another line to produce four irritants: "Domina irata / fumus, et ratta / patella perforata / damnum sunt in casa" [An angry woman, smoke, and a rat, a pan with holes, are ruinous in a house]. The ME translator softens *damnum* to "unprofytable."

4.47a   *Saye not to thy frende.* [B 80a] Proverbs 3:28, "Say not to thy friend: Go, and come again: and to morrow I will give to thee: when thou canst give at present" ["Ne dicas amico tuo: Vade, et revertere, cras dabo tibi, cum statim possis dare"].

4.48a   *He that is wyne dronken holdyth nothing that he sayth.* [B 82a] Compare Ecclesiasticus 20:7, "A wise man will hold his peace till he see opportunity: but a babbler, and a fool, will regard no time" ["Homo sapiens tacebit usque ad tempus; lascivus autem et inprudens non servabunt tempus"].

4.48b   *An opyn arse hath no lord.* [B 82b] Ziolkowski (*Solomon and Marcolf*, pp. 164–65) cites Latin parallels to suggest that the thought here might once have been that it is not possible to control the farting of a *culus confractus* or "opyn arse." Certainly, the arsehole and the fart are frequent topics in Marcolf's discourse, especially as represented by the fullest manuscripts. Equally Marcolfian is the antiauthoritarian ideal of having "no master" or "no lord." The connection to Solomon's pronouncement may be that neither the drunken man nor the "opyn arse" submits to censorship or restraint — an undesirable state from Solomon's perspective, but a positive image of freedom from Marcolf's.

4.50b   *The pore had ne breed and yet he bought an hownde.* [B 84b] Implied criticism of the poor man who buys a dog or feeds his dog before himself is Marcolf's cynical response to Solomon's apparent praise of the poor man who feeds his wife before himself. Whiting indexes Marcolf's remark as P300 with no other instances, but a closely related saying is H564, "the hound eats what the poor man saves," found in a bilingual proverb collection of c. 1300: "hund eet, that hen man spelat / 'Sepe vorat gnarus canis id quod servat avarus.'" Kemble (*Dialogue of Salomon and Saturnus*, p. 63) lists other related sayings.

4.51a   *The fole answeryth aftyr hys folisshnes.* [B 85a] Proverbs 26:5, "Answer a fool according to his folly, lest he imagine himself to be wise" ["Responde stulto juxta stultitiam suam, ne sibi sapiens esse videatur"]. Leeu's Latin text and the ME translation, however, state that the fool *himself* responds according to his foolishness, lest he seem to be wise [to others].

4.51b   *What the stone heryth, that shalle the oke answere.* [B 85b] Benary's edition reads "Petra quod audit, illi respondet echo" [What the stone hears, to that the echo responds]. The Latin prints substitute an oak [*quercus*] for the echo. Whiting's entry S788 cites no other instances but refers the reader to the related expression "to preach to the post" (P317), which suggests a possible interpretation for Marcolf's cryptic remark as we have it here: like the post, the stone hears nothing, not even Solomon's moralizing, and the oak answers nothing back, a negative situation from Solomon's point of view but one that suits Marcolf admirably.

4.52a   *Wrathe hath no mercy.* [B 86a] Proverbs 27:4, "Anger hath no mercy, nor fury when it breaketh forth: and who can bear the violence of one provoked?" ["Ira non habet misericordiam nec erumpens furor; et impetum concitati ferre quis poterit?"].

4.53a   *mouthe of an ennemye.* [B 87a] Compare Proverbs 26:24, "An enemy is known by his lips, when in his heart he entertaineth deceit" ["Labiis suis intelligitur inimicus, cum in corde tractaverit dolos"].

4.54a   *Slepe as ye have nede.* [B 92a] Compare Proverbs 6:4, "Give not sleep to thy eyes, neither let thy eyelids slumber" ["Ne dederis somnum oculis tuis, nec dormitent palpebrae tuae"].

4.55ab–56ab   *We have well fyllyd oure bellys, lete us thanke God . . . as wele as the full fedd.* [B 93ab–94ab] These two exchanges on hunger articulate important themes of the whole dialogue. Solomon speaks from the point of view of the feaster, whose present pleasure helps to console him for the sorrowful knowledge that one day he must die, as at 1 Corinthians 15:32, "Let us eat and drink, for to morrow we shall die" ["Manducemus, et bibamus, cras enim moriemur"]. Marcolf points out that the hungry and the well-fed do not sing the same song (or see the world from the same perspective) and that, like the feasters, the hungry also die, but without the consolation of banquets and merrymaking. The "ouzel/owsell" (L *merulus* [blackbird]) who sings joyfully (*jubilat*) suggests Solomon, whose songs [*carmina*] numbered "a thousand and five" (3 Kings 4:32). Benary's edition reads "respondit ei cuculus" [the cuckoo answered him] — this harsh-voiced respondent suggests Marcolf, whose brash "song" does indeed contrast sharply with Solomon's language. The Latin prints give *graculus* [jackdaw] for *cuculus*, which sustains the idea of a harsh-voiced bird, such as a crow, jay, or grackle. The ME translator's choice of *thrusshe* blunts the contrast somewhat, as it usually indicates a songbird.

4.57a   *Indicte.* [B 95a] ME *indicte* [to write, compose], here, perhaps, a song. L *palogisare* in the Leeu print is unattested, though *paralogizari* [reason falsely] occurs, but this sense seems inappropriate. Benary prints *parabolisare*, which he takes to mean "speak artfully"; it could also mean "speak in proverbs."

4.59a   *Dyspyse thou not a lytyll yifte that is yeven thee of a trewe frende.* [B 97a] While most of Solomon's sententious remarks come from scripture, Benary's edition has at this point a distich derived from the *Distichs of Cato*, a medieval schooltext: "Exiguum munus cum dat tibi pauper amicus / Accipito placite et plene laudare memento" [When a poor friend gives you a meager gift, accept it graciously and remember to praise it heartily]. Leeu's Latin print contains the first line, but the second is abbreviated to "noli despicere" [do not scorn it]. Many proverbs, medieval and modern, testify to the wisdom of appreciating even a small gift and valuing the generosity behind it above the value of the gift.

4.59b   *That a geldyd man hath, that yevyth he to his neigborwes.* [B 97b] As so often, Marcolf's reply is cryptic, and varying interpretations have been offered. The ME translator makes *vicine sue* plural ("his neigborwes"), though the Latin is grammatically singular: "What the castrated man has, he gives to his female neighbor." This could possibly be a wry way of saying that (as a sex partner) the castrated man has *nothing* to give to his female neighbor. Ziolkowski (Solomon and Marcolf, p. 171) suggests that the castrated man "satisfies his [female] neighbor as best he can." Beecher (*Dialogue of Solomon and Marcolphus,* p. 208n62) proposes to emend *castratus* [castrated] to *crassatus* [foolish], suggesting that "what a dim wit owns he gives away."

4.60a   *Go thou not wyth the evyll man or the brawelyng.* [B 99a] Compare Ecclesiasticus 8:18, "Go not on the way with a bold man, lest he burden thee with his evils: for he goeth according to his own will, and thou shalt perish together with his folly" ["Cum audace non eas in via, ne forte gravet mala sua in te; ipse enim secundum voluntatem suam vadit, et simul cum stultitia illius peries"].

4.60b   *A dede bee makyth no hony.* [B 99b] The Latin print uses a coarser expression, "A dead bee does not shit [*caccat*] honey." Whiting B171 offers no other medieval examples but provides cross-references to postmedieval proverb collections.

4.61a   *frendeshipe with a false and evylwylled man.* [B 100a] Proverbs 16:29, "An unjust man allureth his friend: and leadeth him into a way that is not good" ["Vir iniquus lactat amicum suum; et ducit eum per viam non bonam"].

4.62a   *He that answeryth afore he is demaundyd shewyth hymself a fole.* [B 101a] Proverbs 18:13, "He that answereth before he heareth sheweth himself to be a fool, and worthy of confusion" ["Qui prius respondet quam audiat, stultum se esse demonstrat, et confusione dignum"].

4.62b   *tredyth.* [B 101b] L *pungit* [poke, prod]. Beecher (*Dialogue of Solomon and Marcolphus,* p. 208n64) takes Marcolf's advice to mean "when someone is pestering you, leave," which is an acceptable meaning of *retrahere pedem* [depart, withdraw]. Ziolkowski (*Solomon and Marcolf,* p. 172) suggests that the retracting of the foot is in order to kick. That is, if you are poked, you draw back your foot to retaliate. The ME translator apparently takes the prodding to refer to treading on one's foot: if it looks as though someone will step on your foot, you prudently pull it back, a thought consistent with Marcolf's wary self-preservation.

4.63ab   *Evrything chesyth his lyke.* [B 102ab] Ecclesiasticus 13:19, "Every beast loveth its like; so also every man that is nearest to himself" ["omne animal diligit similem sibi sic et omnis homo proximum sibi"]. Variations on the idea that "Everything is attracted to its like" are widespread in medieval proverb tradition. For many English examples, see Whiting L272 (Marcolf's particular expression about scabby horses is indexed as H523 with no other examples). Marcolf's cynical response contests the ideal offered by Solomon, that man and beast each love the others of its kind, and he uses yet another animal image to remind the reader of man's animal body and its susceptibility to disease (the horses are "skabbyd"). The *MED* notes that the rare verb *gnappen* is used by Robert Mannyng to describe tormented people who "gnapped" their own feet and hands as dogs do when they gnaw at their leads; the context here suggests that the horses snap at one another, further contradicting Solomon's idealistic claim that like is affectionate toward like.

4.64a   *A mercyfull man doth wele to his sowle.* [B 103a] Proverbs 11:17, "A merciful man doth good to his own soul" ["Benefacit animae suae vir misericors"].

4.64b   *He dyspyseth a great yifte that knowyth not hymself.* [B 103b] Whiting G73 gives no other examples of Marcolf's particular wording, but the implicit injunction, "Know thyself," K100, is one of the oldest and most common of European proverbs. It seems noteworthy that Marcolf, not Solomon, utters this significant piece of proverbial wisdom. Its message resonates with Marcolf's gibes at Solomon's self-aggrandizement: see for example 4.3ab, 4.6ab, 4.76ab, 7.7–10.

4.65ab   *He that skapyth the wolf metyth the lyon. / From evyll into worse, as the cooke to a bakere.* [B 104ab] See Ziolkowski (*Solomon and Marcolf*, p. 173) for the Aesopian associations of Marcolf's reply. A modern equivalent is "out of the frying pan and into the fire."

4.66b   *The stylle standyng watyr and the man that spekyth but lytylle, beleve thaym not.* [B 105b] A widespread medieval proverb. Singer (*Sprichwörter*, 1:54) notes its presence in the *Distichs of Cato* 4.31. Whiting gives many variants on the well-known expression "still waters run deep" (W70); he indexes Marcolf's particular version separately as W63 with references to postmedieval proverb collections. The proverb warns against still waters because they can conceal unsuspected depths or hazards; metaphorically it urges caution in dealing with people who keep their thoughts to themselves.

4.67b   *in a boke.* [B 106b] L *in casibus* from *casus* [fall; incident; case; misfortune]. The ME translator, understandably perplexed about the author's intent, has chosen a meaning to fit the context. Benary's edition has "in breve" [in brief]. The ME translation thus creates a rare instance of Marcolf citing from books.

4.68ab   *A chylde of an hundred yere . . . It is to late an olde hounde in a bande to lede.* [B
         110ab] Solomon's prophetic injunction is a variation on Isaias 65:20, "There
         shall no more be an infant of days there, nor an old man that shall not fill up
         his days: for the child shall die a hundred years old, and the sinner being a
         hundred years old shall be accursed" ["non erit ibi amplius infans dierum, et
         senex qui non impleat dies suos, quoniam puer centum annorum morietur,
         et peccator centum annorum maledictus erit"]. Marcolf replies with a homely
         observation about the difficulty of training an old dog to the leash for which
         Singer (*Sprichwörter*, 1:51–52) gives numerous Latin analogues. The modern
         equivalent is of course the familiar saying, "You can't teach an old dog new
         tricks."

4.69a   *He that hath, shal be yeven, and shall flowe.* [B 111a] Matthew 25:29, "For to
         every one that hath shall be given, and he shall abound" ["Omni enim
         habenti dabitur, et abundabit"]; also Matthew 13:12.

4.70ab   *hath a dowble herte. . . that wolle two weyes go.* [B 113ab] Ecclesiasticus 2:14,
         "Woe to them that are of a double heart and to wicked lips, and to the hands
         that do evil, and to the sinner that goeth on the earth two ways" ["Vae duplici
         corde, et labiis scelestis, et manibus malefacientibus, et peccatori terram
         ingredienti duabus viis"]; also 3:28. In this amusing pairing, Solomon's mono-
         logic belief in a single path toward a single truth is undercut by Marcolf's
         literal warning against the anatomical and sartorial hazards of walking in two
         directions at once. In exchange 4.72ab, Marcolf again uses the human
         backside to make a point about singularity and doubleness.

4.71a   *Of habundaunce of th'erte the mouth spekyst.* [B 116a] Matthew 12:34 and Luke
         6:45, "For out of the abundance of the heart the mouth speaketh" ["ex
         abundantia enim cordis os loquitur"].

4.73a   *A fayre woman is to be lovyd of hire husbande.* [B 118a] Compare Ecclesiasticus
         26:21, "As the sun when it riseth to the world in the high places of God, so is
         the beauty of a good wife for the ornament of her house" ["sicut sol oriens
         mundo in altissimis Dei sic mulieris bonae species in ornamentum domus
         ejus"]; Proverbs 12:4, "A diligent woman is a crown to her husband" ["Mulier
         diligens corona est viro suo"].

4.73b   *derke.* [B 118b] L *irsuta* is "hairy, shaggy" rather than "dark."

4.75a   *Nede makyth a right wyse man to do evyll.* [B 120a] Compare Ecclesiastes 7:21,
         "For there is no just man upon earth, that doth good, and sinneth not" ["Non
         est enim homo justus in terra qui faciat bonum et non peccet"].

4.76b   *katte.* [B 122b] The ME translator's rendering of L *catulus* [puppy].

4.77b   *The glouton kan not se or renne al aboute.* [B 123b] The meaning of the L "Gluto
         non currit per totum" [The glutton does not run through everything] is
         unclear. Benary's edition has "non comedit" [does not eat] in place of "non
         currit" [does not run], but the thought would make better sense without the
         negative *non* (i.e., "the glutton eats through everything"), as Ziolkowski points

out (*Solomon and Marcolf*, p. 182). The ME translator seems to imagine vision and mobility problems resulting from gluttony.

4.78b   *The shepherde that wakyth welle, ther shall the wolf no wolle shyte.* [B 124b] An attentive shepherd does not fall asleep and leave his sheep to be eaten by wolves, who therefore do not excrete the sheep's wool. The ME translator produces the right sense despite an erroneous Latin text: "Molli bergario lupus non cacat lanam" [When the shepherd is lax, the wolf does not shit wool]. This proverb was widely used in medieval works as a criticism of bad supervision or leadership. Singer (*Sprichwörter*, 1:48–49) gives analogues for the Latin expression, and Whiting S241 and S242 offer parallels from Langland and Chaucer. The C-text of Langland's *Piers Plowman* gives versions in both ME and Latin that resemble Marcolf's saying quite closely: "Thyne sheep are ner al shabbyd [covered with sores], the wolf shiteth woolle. "Sub molli pastore lupus lanam cacat" (Passus 10, line 264). Chaucer's Physician's Tale uses a sanitized version of the expression to chide lax parents: "Under a shepherde softe and necligent / The wolf hath many a sheep and lamb torent [torn apart]" (*CT* VI[C]101–02).

4.79a   *It becomth no foles to speke or to brynge forth any wyse reason.* [B 126a] Proverbs 17:7, "Eloquent words do not become a fool" ["Non decent stultum verba composita"].

4.79b   *It becomyth not a dogge to bere a sadylle.* [B 126b] A widespread proverbial comparison ridicules an inappropriate form of human behavior (such as the dispensing of wisdom by a fool mentioned by Solomon in 4.79a) by evoking the image of a saddle worn by an inappropriate animal: Whiting S533 cites a version with a sow and C501 features a cow. For Latin examples, see Ziolkowski, *Solomon and Marcolf*, pp. 183–84.

4.80a   *Whyles the children are lytyll, reighte theyre lymmes and maners.* [B 127a] Compare Ecclesiasticus 30:12, "beat his sides while he is a child" ["tunde latera ejus dum infans est"].

4.82a   *Of a good man comth a good wyf.* [B 130b] The sentiment is close to Ecclesiasticus 26:3, "A good wife is a good portion, she shall be given in the portion of them that fear God, to a man for his good deeds" ["Pars bona mulier bona, in parte timentium Deum dabitur viro pro factis bonis"].

4.82b   *alle the bestyalle wyves trede undre fote.* [B 130b] One of the ugliest antifeminist images in the print versions of the dialogue. An ample meal produces an ample turd that men trample under foot, just as they should trample "bestiales mulieres" [bestial women]. The ME print has an overturned *u* in *wyues* that makes the word look like *wynes*. Overturned *u*'s and *n*'s are a common typesetting error in the ME text, as our textual notes witness.

4.84b   *hepe of stonys.* [B 132b] Leeu's Latin print has *strues* [stack, heap], where most manuscripts have *strontus* [turd]. Perhaps this was a sanitizing gesture, though ample scatology remains. The phrase "of stonys" is the ME translator's addition. This pairing (4.84ab) is a good reminder that the term *proverb* applies only very loosely to a number of the remarks in this verbal contest. Marcolf's rejoinder is a close verbal parody of Solomon's reference to his sword, a symbol of his aristocratic position in the social hierarchy, which Marcolf reduces to a mundane barnyard image. A house and shed surrounded by a hedge was a characteristic peasant dwelling in medieval Europe, and the pile of dung mentioned by the manuscript versions would be no uncommon sight. A similar but more transgressive pairing (B 40ab in Appendix) is omitted from the prints: there Solomon evokes another symbol of aristocratic status by declaring that a black boss fits perfectly on a white shield; Marcolf replies that a black arsehole sits perfectly between white cheeks.

4.85a   *The gretter that ye be, the more meke shulde ye be in alle thyngys.* [B 133a] Ecclesiasticus 3:20, "The greater thou art, the more humble thyself in all things" ["Quanto magnus es, humilia te in omnibus"].

4.85b   *He rydyth well that ridyth wyth his felawes.* [B 133b] For "wyth his felawes," Leeu's Latin print gives *cum paribus* [with his equals]; this is probably the import of the ME expression as well.

4.86a   *The wyse chylde gladyth the fadyr.* [B 136a] Proverbs 10:1, "A wise son maketh the father glad: but a foolish son is the sorrow of his mother" ["Filius sapiens laetificat patrem; filius vero stultus moestitia est matris suae"].

4.87a   *He that sowyth wyth skaerstye repyth skaersly* [B 137a]. 2 Corinthians 9:6, "He who soweth sparingly, shall also reap sparingly" ["Qui parce seminat, parce et metet"].

4.88a, 89a   *Do alle thynges by counsell. . . . Alle thinges have theyre seasons and tyme.* [B 139a, 140a] Solomon appears to play his strongest cards just as the match ends: these two biblical sayings are among the most widely cited pieces of Solomonic wisdom in medieval literature. In English alone, Whiting records about twenty citations of the advice from Ecclesiasticus 32:24, "Do thou nothing without counsel" (C470) and a similar number for Ecclesiastes 3:1, "All things have their season [time]" (T88).

4.89b   *Now daye; tomorwe daye.* [B 140b] The Latin "Diem hodie, diem cras" might be translated "Today is a day, tomorrow is [another] day," with the implication "there is always tomorrow, if I don't succeed today," an expression of resignation appropriate to a lumbering ox who tries to catch a hare. Singer (*Sprichwörter,* 1:49–50) gives parallels.

5.2   *thyrdde in the kingedome.* [B Epil.] At Daniel 5:16 and 29, King Belshazaar promises Daniel that he will make him the "third prince" in the kingdom, if he can read and interpret the writing on the wall.

5.5   *Quare rex promisit?* [B Epil.] Immediately preceding in the Latin text is another question, "Quis adheret culo nisi pastelli?" [Who sticks to the arsehole except little clots?]. *Pastellus* is "pastry; pastille," but the meaning is unclear. This obscure question is omitted from the ME text.

5.6   *kinges xii provostes.* [B Epil.] The list of Solomon's governors is based on 3 Kings 4:7–19. There is considerable variation in spellings and one governor, Achimaas (Leeu's "Achimaab"), is missing from the English.

5.8   *Why dryve ye hym not out . . . of his syghte?* [B Epil.] At beginning of 5.8, the phrase "Cur non magnis colaphis maceratur" [Why isn't he tormented with great blows?] is omitted from the ME.

5.11   *There is no king were no lawe is.* [B Epil.] For other reproofs of Solomon's kingship, see note to 11.7 and see also 13.7, where Marcolf again responds to what he considers an act of injustice: "where as the hede is seke and evyll at ease, there is no lawe."

6–8   [B 2.1–3] The riddling contest. In sections 6 through 8, the scene moves from Solomon's court to Marcolf's peasant house, imagined as sufficiently close by for the king and his men to come upon it while hunting. On his home ground, Marcolf takes the lead by posing riddles, just as Solomon led off in the exchanges of genealogies and proverbs that took place at his court. Figure 5 depicts the answers to each of Marcolf's riddles, as they are given in 6.6–9 and 6.16–20. For analogues to these riddles, see Ziolkowski, *Solomon and Marcolf,* pp. 196–99. Solomon's lack of success in solving Marcolf's riddles presumably arises from his lack of experiential knowledge. The solutions involve basic realities of peasant life: preparing food, raising crops, fighting off vermin, preparing a body for burial, and conceiving a child. Bakhtin observes that riddles can transform life's most terrifying mysteries into a "gay and carefree" game (*Rabelais,* p. 233).

6.16   *footpath.* [B 2.1] The path apparently runs through the father's crops. When he sets out thorns to deflect pedestrians from one harmful or destructive path, they trample another.

7.1–10   [B 2.2] The origins of Solomon's wisdom and Marcolf's cleverness. This intriguing etiological tale, nestled between the two parts of the riddling match, begins with Solomon's demand for an explanation of the unexpected wit he discovers in this coarse rustic. Scholars have noted a mild anomaly in the narrative frame, in that Marcolf seems to arrive as a stranger to Solomon when the work opens, and now we have a flashback to a past in which Marcolf was present when Solomon's mother prepared her son the vulture's heart that gave him his extraordinary wisdom. That Barsebea roasted the heart on a piece of bread and "gave" it to Solomon to eat (L *tibi comedere dedit*, ME "yave you the herte to ete"), but only afterward threw the uneaten crust to Marcolf (L *projecit*, ME "kast at my hede"), suggests that Marcolf may simply have been a hungry boy lurking about the royal kitchen who received little attention from either Solomon or his mother and need not have been recognizable as an adult to his sovereign. Solomon denies the truth of Marcolf's tale in 7.7, unsurprisingly preferring the biblical account in which his wisdom was God-given rather than a result of his mother's sorcery (see 3 Kings 3:4–15). Marcolf makes up a number of self-serving fictions over the course of the work, and this one too may be a tall tale, not to be taken literally as part of the framing narrative. Marcolf's hunger has symbolic resonance throughout the work, and in 8.17 he again implies that his hunger and his cleverness are related.

7.2   *there was a yonge man his phisician.* [B 2.2] The physicians of the Latin text (*medici*) become a single physician in ME.

8.2–3   *pot of the same cowe be coveryd.* [B 2.3] Here Solomon rashly offers a riddle of his own: he requests a pot of milk "covered" by the cow that produced the milk. Marcolf's mother, Floscemya, readily offers a solution: she covers the milk with a flat cake (L *placenta*) or, in English, a flan, also prepared with the milk of the family cow. Marcolf discomfits Solomon with an alternate solution: a "drye bakyn cowe torde" also allows one to cover the jug of milk with the product of the same cow.

8.14–15   *I commaunded not so to be done. . . Thus I undyrstode.* [B II.3] Solomon's insistence and Marcolf's rejoinder once again emphasize the difference in perspective between the two, the difficulties they face in communicating across contrastive discourses, and Marcolf's deliberate exploitation of this gap in communication.

8.17   *hungyr chaungyd wyt.* [B 2.3] The ME translator may have chosen this literal rendition of "fames mutavit ingenium" as a way of acknowledging the Latin text's play on the meanings of *ingenium* here and in 8.20 ("pro ipso ingenio"), where the word also applies to Marcolf and can mean either by his "wit" or by his "clever contrivance or stratagem" (see Cosquin, "Le Conte du chat," pp. 390–91). For discussions of *ingenium* or cleverness as a controversial intellectual faculty, see Hanning, *Individual in Twelfth-Century Romance,* especially pp. 105–38, and Blamires, "Women and Creative Intelligence." For Marcolf's *ingenium,* contrasted with Solomon's received wisdom, as a source of the dialogue's unity and dynamism, see Bradbury, "Rival Wisdom."

8.20   *the pot I have thus coveryd wyth a cowe torde.* [B 2.3] Marcolf has the last laugh in the riddling match, just as he prevails in 4.91ab at the end of the proverb contest. Solomon's lack of success at posing his own riddle seems to arise from the same problem that impeded him in answering Marcolf's riddles: he lacks sufficient awareness of the openness of language to multiple interpretations as well as a knowledge of the gritty barnyard realities of peasant life. In envisioning an appetizing solution to the "covered by the same cow" riddle, Solomon thinks of the kind of milk-glazed delicacy someone prepares for him but not of the dung produced by the cow.

9.1–13.8   Propositions and proofs. Sections 9 through 13 [B 2.4–8] present a contest within a contest. Growing annoyed with Marcolf, Solomon condemns him to beheading if he cannot stay awake all night (9.1). Each time Solomon accuses him of sleeping, Marcolf responds with a proposition, and Solomon demands that he prove it, again on pain of death.

9.17   *wery of waking.* [B 2.4] After challenging Marcolf to stay awake all night in 9.1, at the end of the night Solomon grows "wery of waking," just as he grew "wery of spekyng" at the end of the proverb contest (4.90a). In the hyper-polarized world of the *Dialogue*, the emphasis on Solomon's weariness may imply that he represents an ancient, fixed, canonical tradition that is running out of precepts and out of energy, whereas Marcolf possesses the energy of newer discourses gaining ground over the course of the Middle Ages with their capacity to improvise, challenge authority, and foster change. See Corti, "Models and Antimodels in Medieval Culture," and Bradbury, "Rival Wisdom."

10.1   *hys sustyr Fudasa*. [B 2.5] The sister of Marcolf is first mentioned without name in the riddle contest as weeping over her unwed pregnancy (6.19–20); here she is given the name Fudasa (Fusada in Benary's edition). As a result of the pregnancy, she is "thycker than she was of lenghthe" (12.4), and she also bears an unfortunate resemblance to Marcolf in the face (*vysage*, 12.5), much to Solomon's amusement when he first sees her in 12.3. Marcolf's face is caricatured in 2.2–5.

10.2   *The king Salomon is ayenst me*. [B 2.5] The ME translation of Marcolf's statement, "Rex Salomon contrarius est mihi," conveys the primary meaning of the statement in context. Given the academic language of this section (the repetition of the verb *probare* [prove]), a possible secondary meaning is "King Solomon is contrary to me," in the sense of an opposite or logical contrary, another reminder of the polarized nature of this entire dialogue between king and peasant and of the many oppositions the two represent. The importance of contraries, contradictions, and opposites in medieval literature has been the subject of extensive scholarship: see Solterer, *Master and Minerva*; Brown, *Contrary Things*; Sarah Kay, *Courtly Contradictions*; and Bouchard, "*Every Valley Shall Be Exalted*."

11.5   *he stumblyd at the panne and was nygh fallyn therin*. [B 2.6] Solomon's stumble causes him, in his own words, nearly to break his neck (11.8). The inversion of his words of wisdom in the proverb contest now becomes a literal near-inversion of his royal person. The comic upending (or the thrashing or uncrowning) of a king was for Bakhtin a carnivalesque image that offers a symbolic "element of victory" for the popular spirit over official forces of authority and intimidation, "the defeat of power, of earthly kings, of the earthly upper classes, of all that oppresses and restricts" (*Rabelais*, p. 92; see also pp. 197–208).

11.7   *Juge egaly* (i.e., "judge impartially"). [B 2.6] Solomon is of course famed for his just judgments, most notably that between the two women who claim to be the mother of the same child, mentioned at 4.5a and 16.1–4. As part of the comic inversion enacted by this work, Marcolf "schools" the king in what should be Solomon's own virtues by asking him to rule justly (here and in 11.9) and with patience (12.23). In Benary's edition (II.9), Marcolf implicitly chides Solomon for the lack of mercy [*misericordia*] shown to him at court. See 5.11 and 13.7 for more criticism of Solomon's kingship.

12.20   *thou doost alle thy thynges by crafte and subtyltye* [B 2.7]. Solomon's remark calls attention once again to Marcolf's central characteristic, his amoral cleverness.

13　　*in the kinges house a catte . . . wont to holde . . . a brennyng kandell.* [B 2.8–9] For Marcolf's proof of the fifth and final proposition of this contest, that nature wins out over nurture, the author draws upon a widespread folktale that can also take the form of an exemplum or a proverb. For the dispersion of "the cat and the candle" motif, see Cosquin, "Le Conte du chat"; Beecher, ed., *Dialogue of Solomon and Marcolphus*, pp. 215–16n106; Ben-Amos, *Folktales of the Jews*, 1:397–404; and Ziolkowski, *Solomon and Marcolf*, pp. 217–18. In "The Story of the Cat and the Candle in Middle English Literature," Braekman and Macaulay edit and comment on a related ME dialogue between "Kynd" [Nature] and "Nurtur," in which Nurtur owns the carefully trained cat and tries to use it to "preve that nurtur passis kynd," only to be refuted by Kynd, who employs a mouse in the same way that Marcolf does. (See also V. J. Scattergood, "'Debate between Nurture and Kynd'" for the ME dialogue and some literary relations.) In the ME poem, found in London, British Library, MS Harley 541, fols. 212v–213r, the roles of Nurtur and Kynd correspond intriguingly to those represented by the two interlocutors in our prose dialogue. Solomon's innumerable moral precepts and the schoolmasterish persona given him in the various versions of our dialogue make him ideally suited to defend the side of Nurtur, education or "lernyng," as the ME translator calls it in 9.16 and 13.5. In contrast, Marcolf's investment in nature (inborn qualities) over nurture (learned behavior) follows from his necessary reliance on his native wit in the absence of formal education. In our dialogue, Solomon carefully trains the cat and Marcolf takes advantage of its instincts and appetites.

13.8　　*Neythre so nor so shall the wyse Salomon of Marcolf be quyte.* [B 2.8] Marcolf's assertion that Solomon will never be rid of him reminds the reader of the persistence of the values for which Marcolf stands, including the needs, appetites, and instincts of the body and man's necessary connection to the natural world. The ME translator does not render the epithet *britone / bricone* [rogue, scoundrel] applied to Marcolf in Leeu's Latin text.

15.1–10　　*spytte not but upon the bare grownde.* [B 2.10] Marcolf's claim that his spit will benefit the bald man's head by fertilizing it (making it "fat") so that hair can grow echoes the language of 4.16b, his longest contribution to the proverb contest, where he stresses the fertilizing benefit that the waste products of an ass offer to a field.

15.12　　*Balydnesse is a flyes nest.* [B 2.10] L *muscarum ludibrium* is literally 'butt of jokes for flies.' Ziolkowski notes that the attraction bald heads hold for flies is a familiar motif in fables (*Solomon and Marcolf*, p. 224).

15.15　　*And be it pease in thy vertu.* [B 2.10] Psalm 121:7, "Let peace be in thy strength" ["Fiat pax in virtute tua"].

16.1–4　　*two women bryngyng wyth thaym a lyving chylde.* [B 2.11] The famous judgment of Solomon between two women who lay claim to the same child, very much as narrated in 3 Kings 3:16–27. In 18.1–4 below, Marcolf deliberately misrepresents Solomon's intentions toward the child as part of his campaign to make Solomon contradict his speech in praise of women.

17.3–7 *Ye myghthe so be disceyved.* [B 2.12] Here, as in the proverb contest, the two speakers trade conventional remarks in praise and blame of women. An excellent introduction to the primary sources of this ongoing medieval debate is Blamires, ed., *Woman Defamed and Woman Defended.* Versions of the saying that "Women can weep with one eye and laugh with the other" were proverbial in English (Whiting W538) and appear in Chaucer, *Book of the Duchess,* lines 633–34, and Robert Henryson, "The Testament of Cresseid" (*Poems,* ed. Elliott), lines 230–31. The other antifeminist sentiments Marcolf expresses here regarding women's propensity for deceit and manipulation were also familiar in Latin and in the vernaculars. For ME examples, see Whiting W495, W498, W505, W508 and W532.

17.15–16 *'weyke erthe' or a 'weyke thynge.'* [B 2.12] In Leeu's Latin text, Solomon states that the word for woman, *mulier,* derives from *mollis res* [soft thing] (*mollis aer* [soft air] occurs in some manuscripts). The ME text renders *mollis res* with a doublet, "a 'weyke erthe' or a 'weyke thynge.'" Ziolkowski (*Solomon and Marcolf,* p. 228) notes that Isidore of Seville, following Varro, derived *mulier* from *mollities* [softness] in his vastly influential *Etymologies.* Marcolf retorts that *mollis error* [soft mistake] would be a more apt derivation.

17.26 *thinkyth wyth his herte as he spekyth wyth his mowth.* [B 2.12] The thought is related to Matthew 12:34 and Luke 6:45, "out of the abundance of the heart the mouth speaketh" ["ex abundantia enim cordis os loquitur"].

17.28 *or ye slepe ye shal dysprayse thaym.* [B 2.12] Marcolf initiates the final verbal contest by boasting that Solomon will soon dispraise women as strongly as he praised them in 17.18–25. This last contest draws upon the ancient and medieval rhetorical practices of crafting arguments on both sides of an issue [*in utramque partem*] and composing elaborate speeches of praise and blame. Solomon will in fact deliver two more speeches on women, one of blame (21.1–7) and one of praise (23.4–10). The final speeches of blame and praise are a tissue of scriptural citations from Ecclesiasticus 25–26, quoted verbatim (or nearly so). Ecclesiasticus was attributed to Solomon in the Middle Ages, and thus the self-contradiction in which Marcolf traps Solomon in this dialogue also reveals self-contradiction in the supposed biblical writings of Solomon, another example of the work's irreverent stance toward holy writ.

18.1–15 *thou shalt have the one half of thy chylde and thy felawe the othre half . . . evyr man shall have vii wyves.* [B 2.13] Marcolf's account of Solomon's planned injustices to women is of course a web of lies spun to goad his female subjects into rebellion against the king so that he will veer from extreme praise of women to equally extreme blame, as Marcolf has promised. The fictions Marcolf weaves in order to win this verbal contest resemble the earlier deceptions he practiced in order to exasperate his sister Fudasa into breaking her promise, thereby supporting Marcolf's contention that a woman's word cannot be trusted. That Solomon can only quote the culture's central canonical text while

Marcolf improvises amoral but imaginative new fictions situates the two speakers at the extremes of yet another polarity.

18.14   *many great inconvenyencys shall growe thereof.* [B 2.13] A softened version of the Latin "una preparabit alteri venenum" [one will prepare poison against the other].

19.4   *vi thousand women.* [B 2.14] Leeu's Latin text reads *septem milia mulierum* [seven thousand women]. The ME print reads *vi. Mi.,* presumably a typesetting error.

20.7   *Wherefore do ye unryght?* [B 2.15] The criticism of Solomon's kingship by his infuriated female subjects echoes Marcolf's own earlier reproofs in 5.11, 11.7, and 13.7 above. Even one of Solomon's loyal councilors joins this chorus of criticism in 22.1–3.

20.10   *For there is not that prynce . . . but that oon woman alone shall now fullfylle alle his desyres and wylle.* [B 2.15] Leeu's Latin text seems to mean that no man is so wealthy or powerful that he could fulfill in [even] one single wife [all] her desires ["qui uni soli uxori suas impleat voluntates"]. How then will he handle multiple wives? The ME text assigns the desires to the man but keeps to the point that one wife is enough for any man: no man is so wealthy or powerful that his desires cannot be met by a single woman.

20.13   *youre sentences ben false and unrightfull.* [B 2.15] ME "sentences" = L *sentencie;* in context the primary meaning is Solomon's judicial sentences or royal proclamations, but in both languages "sentences" also applies to the pro-verbial wisdom spoken by Solomon in the proverb contest and throughout the dialogue. Since Solomon's reputation rests on his excellence in both areas, Marcolf tricks the women into verbalizing a direct attack on Solomon's standing as just king and wisdom figure.

20.15   *now this Salomon werst of alle.* [B 2.15] Another direct hit at Solomon's prestige is this attack on his patriarchal lineage. Just as Marcolf parodies the solemn series of "begats" recited by Solomon in 4.2a by rehearsing a disreputable list of his own mock-ancestors in 4.2b, so these angry women invert the positive force of Solomon's royal genealogy by claiming that King Saul was evil, King David worse, and King Solomon worst of all.

21.1–7   *There is no hede more worse. . . wyckyd woman.* [B 2.16] As our biblical citations indicate, Solomon's attack on women is drawn mainly from Ecclesiasticus 25–26, beginning with 25:22–23, "There is no head worse than the head of a serpent: And there is no anger above the anger of a woman. It will be more agreeable to abide with a lion and a dragon, than to dwell with a wicked woman" ["Non est caput nequius super caput colubri, et non est ira super iram mulieris. Commorari leoni et draconi placebit, quam habitare cum muliere nequam"].

21.2–3   *cursydnesse of a shrewd woman . . . sande fallyth in the shoes.* [B 2.16] Ecclesiasticus 25:26–27, "All malice is short to the malice of a woman, let the lot of sinners fall upon her. As the climbing of a sandy way is to the feet of the aged, so is a wife full of tongue to a quiet man" ["Brevis omnis malitia super malitiam mulieris; sors peccatorum cadat super illam. Sicut ascensus arenosus in pedibus veterani, sic mulier linguata homini quieto"].

21.4   *That wyf that is hir husbondes maister is evyr contrarye to hym.* [B 2.16] Ecclesiasticus 25:30, "A woman, if she have superiority, is contrary to her husband" ["Mulier si primatum habeat, contraria est viro suo"].

21.5   *An evyl wyf makyth a pacient herte.* [B 2.16] Ecclesiasticus 25:31, "A wicked woman abateth the courage, and maketh a heavy countenance, and a wounded heart" ["Cor humile, et facies tristis, et plaga cordis, mulier nequam"].

21.6   *begynnyng of synne, and through hire we dye alle.* [B 2.16] Ecclesiasticus 25:33, "From the woman came the beginning of sin, and by her we all die" ["A muliere initium factum est peccati, et per illam omnes morimur"]. At this point, Leeu's Latin print inserts two lines from Ecclesiasticus 26:8–9; these verses are missing in the ME text: "Dolor cordis et luctus mulier zelotypa. In muliere zelotypa flagellum linguae, omnibus communicans" [A jealous woman is the grief and mourning of the heart. With a jealous woman is a scourge of the tongue which communicateth with all].

21.7   *The woman that is luxuriouse.* [B 2.16] The adjective *luxuriouse* [lustful] renders the implications of L *fornicatio.* Ecclesiasticus 26:12–14, "The fornication of a woman shall be known by the haughtiness of her eyes, and by her eyelids. . . . Take heed of the impudence of her eyes, and wonder not if she slight thee" ["Fornicatio mulieris in extollentia oculorum, et in palpebris illius agnoscetur . . . Ab omni irreverentia oculorum ejus cave, et ne mireris si te neglexerit"].

22.5–6   *Now have ye spokyn aftyr myn intent. . . alwayes ye make my saying trewe.* [B 2.17] Marcolf declares victory over Solomon in their last major verbal contest.

22.9   *Betwixt the yes.* [B 2.17] *Betwixt the yes* [Between the eyes] = L *in mediis oculis.* Repeated in 24.1, the idiom "to see someone 'amidst' or 'between' the eyes" receives an interesting twist in the punchline to this jest in 24.12.

23.5–10   [B 2.18] Solomon's praise of women. Like his attack in 21, his praise is a tissue of verses from Ecclesiasticus 26:3, 16–19, 21–24, some cited verbatim, some only approximate. The ME translator gives the general sense of the passage rather than a close translation. Our punctuation of the Latin text follows the Bible, insofar as it is possible.

23.5–6   *For a good wyf makyth hyr husbande glad and blythe . . . a parte the lyvyng of hyre husbond.* [B 2.18] Compare Ecclesiasticus 26:3, "A good wife is a good portion, she shall be given in the portion of them that fear God, to a man for his good deeds" ["Pars bona mulier bona, in parte timentium Deum dabitur viro pro factis bonis"].

23.6–7   *hyr lernyng advauntagyth or forthryth hys body. She is a yifte of God.* [B 2.18] The ME text follows the Latin in making *disciplina* the subject of *impinguabit* [will fatten]. L *disciplina* here is "discipline" rather than "lernyng," as is clear from Ecclesiasticus 26:16–17, "The grace of a diligent woman shall delight her husband, and shall fat his bones. Her discipline is the gift of God" ["gratia mulieris sedulae delectabit virum suum, et ossa illius impinguabit. Disciplina illius datum Dei est"].

23.7   *A wyse wyf and a stylle is a grace aboven graces.* [B 2.18] The line telescopes Ecclesiasticus 26:18–19, "Such is a wise and silent woman, and there is nothing so much worth as a well instructed soul. A holy and shamefaced woman is grace upon grace" ["Mulier sensata et tacita; non est inmutatio eruditae animae. Gratia super gratiam mulier sancta et pudorata"].

23.8–10   *the sonne clymmyng up to God. . . ornament or apparayle of the house. . . lyght shynyng bryghther. . . lyke the goolden pyller. . . the commandemantys of God evyr in hyr mynde* [B 2.18]. Ecclesiasticus 26:21–24, "As the sun when it riseth to the world in the high places of God, so is the beauty of a good wife for the ornament of her house. As the lamp shining upon the holy candlestick, so is the beauty of the face in a ripe age. As golden pillars upon bases of silver, so are the firm feet upon the soles of a steady woman. As everlasting foundations upon a solid rock, so the commandments of God in the heart of a holy woman" ["Sicut sol oriens mundo in altissimis Dei, sic mulieris bonae species in ornamentum domus ejus. Lucerna splendens super candelabrum sanctum, et species faciei super aetatem stabilem. Columnae aureae super bases argenteas, et pedes firmi super plantas stabilis mulieris. Fundamenta aeterna super petram solidam, et mandata Dei in corde mulieris sanctae"].

24.2–3   *a great snowe.* [B 2.19] This heavy snowfall, accepted as a matter of course by Solomon and his councilors, is incongruous with the supposed setting in biblical Jerusalem but consistent with Marcolf's identity as a European peasant. Clearly the sieve and bear paw, like the reversed shoes, are meant to confuse Solomon and his men as they hunt Marcolf, tracking him like an animal. Why he chooses a sieve and bear paw in particular is not explained, but the use of one very human implement and one animal paw suggests the ambiguity of Marcolf's humanity evident from the opening description of him, with its many animal comparisons. The repeated application of the word *beste* to Marcolf emphasizes this ambiguity: "lyke a beste" (24.3), "a merveylous beste" (24.5), "the sayd wondrefull beeste" (24.6).

24.8   *Hys vysage from hymwardes.* [B 2.19] That is, the bent-over Marcolf faces away from Solomon, who is thus confronted with "hys arshole and alle hys othre fowle gere." Without spoiling the joke, the ME text bowdlerizes mildly the corresponding Latin text: "nates, et culus, et curgulio, et testiculi" [cheeks, and arsehole, and penis, and testicles]. Citing J. N. Adams, *The Latin Sexual Vocabulary* (London: Duckworth, 1982), pp. 33–34, Ziolkowski (*Solomon and Marcolf*, p. 240) notes that *curculio* [corn weevil] is used of the penis in Persius, *Satires* 4.38. The Venetian vernacular print edited by Quinto Marini bowdlerizes this passage in a manner similar to the ME text: "le nateghe, el culo e li membra deshoneste" (*Il dialogo di Salomone e Marcolfo*, p. 135).

25.2–6   *yeve me leve to chose the tre wherupon that I shalle hange.* [B 2.20] Marcolf's last jest, yet another verbal quibble, saves his life.

25.7–8   *And thus he askapyd out of the dawnger and handes of King Salomon.* [B 2.20] Benary's text ends with the Latin equivalent of this statement: "Et sic Marcolfus evasit manus regis Salomonis." Ziolkowski aptly calls this abrupt ending "the opposite of closure" (*Solomon and Marcolf,* p. 6); Marcolf simply escapes from his most recent predicament. Interestingly, texts in the print tradition add another clause to give not just closure but a happy ending to Marcolf's adventures: "Post hoc domum remeans quievit in pace" ("And turnyd ayen unto hys howse, and levyd in pease and joye"), the "joye" an addition on the part of the ME translator. The prayer for the salvation of the author and reader appended to the ME text is a common addition to the endings of non-religious texts such as metrical romances.

 TEXTUAL NOTES

ABBREVIATIONS: see Explanatory Notes

The typographical errors silently corrected in the text are listed below with our correction first and then the reading in Leeu's print. Misset letters in the Middle English text (either overturned or reversed) are indicated by italics.

LATIN

4.4a	nominatissimus: nominatissimua
4.10a	ipsa: ipsam
5.6	Hommia: bommia
12.13	Fudasa: Fudasia
12.16	Fudasa: Fudasia

MIDDLE ENGLISH

Title	betwixt: betwxt
Incipit	b*u*t (overturned *u*)
2.1	This: Thls
2.5	of a goet: ef a goet
3.4	yre*n* (overturned *n*)
3.5	She: Se
4.1b	thereto: thereo
	declare yo*u* (overturned *u*)
4.2b	R*u*stum (overturned *u*)
4.2c	that gat: tha gat
4.3a	altercacion: altercacon
4.4a	answere: vnswere
4.6a	yave: yawe
4.8b	potf*u*ll (overturned *u*)
4.10a	shal be: shabbe
4.19b	a*n* axe (overturned *n*)
4.21b	his: is
4.25a	stronge: strõgr
	thou: thau
4.27a	tho*u* (overturned *u*)
4.28b	the bren: te bren

4.32a	maister: maist
4.32b	that she: thath she
	hath: hat
4.34a	cou*n*sell (overturned *u*)
4.38b	more: moee
4.42a	the wycked: he wycked
4.42b	bot*h*e (overturned *h*)
4.43a	he beggyd: be heggyd
4.50a	a*n*d (overturned *n*)
4.51b	the oke: te oke
4.52a	therefore: trefore
4.55a	bellys: beliys
4.62a	shewy*th* (overturned *h*)
4.64a	mercyfull: meycyfull
4.65a	the wolf: te wolf
4.74a	Juda: I*u*da (overturned *u*)
	me: ñ
4.78b	shepherde: shephde
4.82b	wyves: wy*u*es (overturned *u*)
4.83a	S: Salo (overturned *S*)
4.90a	speky*n*g (overturned *n*)
5.1	Ma*r*colf (overturned *r*)
	governaunce: gouernañee
	kynges: kyges
5.6	Ne*n*thur (overturned *n*)
5.9	tha*n* (overturned *n*)
5.10	Tho: To
5.11	king: kipg
6.1	a*n*d fortunyd (overturned *n*)
6.6	declyned: declynedy
6.8	demau*n*ded (overturned *n*)
7.4	feyre: fayre
8.2	le*n*gyr (overturned *n*)
8.17	chaungyd: chamigyd
8.19	anoynted: anyonted
9.2	Marcolph: maccolph (first occurrence)
9.4	tho*u* (overturned *u*)
9.9	to rowte: te rowte
9.10	th'erthe: therhe
9.11	Ye: Ie
9.14	shal be: shal*n*e (overturned and reversed *n* for *b*)
9.16	Marcolph: Marcoph
10.2	inj*u*ries (overturned *u*)
10.4	i*n* any wyse (overturned *n*)
10.6	than: tha
10.7	reto*u*r*n*yd (overturned *u*, overturned *n*)
11.1	ill*u*mined (overturned *u*)

11.2	i*n* his tayle (overturned *n*)
	nombredyd: nombredys
11.4	a*n*d closyd (overturned *n*)
11.9	Nevyrthelesse: Nevyrhtelesse
12.5	fote: bote
12.6	of: af
12.11	bothe: bote
12.12	Marcolph: Marcoph
12.14	parte: parthe
12.16	Fudasa: omitted
13.4	she (second occurrence): he
13.8	th*u*s (overturned *u*)
15.3	Marcolf: Marcof
15.8	Salomon: Saolmon
15.11	a*u*ght (overturned *u*)
	b*u*t (overturned *u*)
15.14	ballyd: bailyd
15.15	vert*u* (overturned *u*)
	shal: shai
16.4	naturall modyr: naturall bodyr
	yeve: jeve
17.6	b*u*t (overturned *u*)
17.10	s*u*che (overturned *u*)
17.19	withoute: whitoute
17.23	dilectacioun: dilectacõn
	or joye: of joye
17.25	withhoute: whithoute
18.1	Marcolphus: Marcolphue
18.3	Marcolph: Marcoph
18.5	Marcolph: Marcoph
18.11	What shall tha*n* (overturned *n*)
18.13	The othyr shall nowe: The othyr shall mowe
	They shal nowe: They shal mowe
	maydenhede: mayndehede
19.4	so: se
20.2	to you: tho you
20.3	as many as: as asmany as
20.6	She answeryd: omitted
20.7	tha*n*e (overturned *n*)
20.9	nowe: mowe
20.10	now: mow
20.13	reaso*n* (overturned *n*)
	a*n*d unrightfull (overturned *n*)
20.14	skor*n*e (overturned *n*)
21.1	dwelle: dvelle
21.2	lytyl to: lytyl tho
21.4	hir: hlr

21.5	is as: it as
22.9	no more: nomere
23.8	condicyons (overturned *c*)
23.10	fundament (overturned *u*)
	wythoute (overturned *u*)
23.11	you and (overturned *n*)
	kynderede: kyndrebede
24.1	Marcolph: Marcoph
24.3	in the (overturned *n*)
	that stode: tyat stode
24.5	a merveylous beste: & merveylous beste
24.6	beeste and (overturned *n*)
24.8	Marcolphus: Marcolpus
	he myght: be myght
24.12	commaunded (overturned *u*)
25.2	will: well
25.4	thens (overturned *n*)
	Jericho: ierirho

🌿 APPENDIX

Proverb exchanges present in the "long" versions of *The Dialogue of Solomon and Marcolf* in the manuscripts but not included in the Latin and vernacular prints:

B 9a   S: Mulier bona super omnia bona, mulier mala super omnia mala; mulier mala
              nec defuncta credatur.
              [A good wife is good beyond all things, a bad wife bad beyond all things; a bad
              wife is not to be trusted even when dead.]

B 9b   M: Frange illi ossa et mitte in fossam, tunc joca securus de morte ejus!
              [Break her bones and throw her in a ditch, then joke about her death, carefree!]

B 15a   S: Subtrahe pedem tuum a muliere litigiosa!
              [Withdraw thy foot from a quarrelsome woman!][1]

B 15b   M: Subtrahe nasum tuum a culo jussoso!
              [Withdraw thy nose from a farting ass!]

B 18a   S: Qui stat, videat ne cadat.
              [He that stands, let him take heed lest he fall.][2]

B 18b   M: Qui offendit pedem, respicit ad lapidem.
              [He that stubs his foot looks back at the stone.]

B 21a   S: Luxuriosa res est vinum, et tumultuosa ebrietas.
              [Wine is a luxurious thing, and drunkenness riotous.][3]

B 21b   M: Jejunus est pauper qui ebrius sibi videtur dives.
              [The poor man is hungry, who when drunk supposes himself rich.]

B 22a   S: Qui expectat, consequitur quod desiderat.
              [He that waits, obtains what he desires.]

---

[1] Compare Proverbs 25:17: "Withdraw thy foot from the house of thy neighbour, lest having his fill he hate thee" ["Subtrahe pedem tuum de domo proximi tui, nequando satiatus oderit te"]; 21:9 and 25:24, "It is better to sit in a corner of the housetop, than with a quarrelsome woman, and in a common house" ["melius est sedere in angulo domatis, quam cum muliere litigiosa, et in domo communi"].

[2] Compare 1 Corinthians 10:12: "Wherefore he that thinketh himself to stand, let him take heed lest he fall" ["Itaque qui se existimat stare, videat ne cadat"].

[3] Proverbs 20:1: "Luxuriosa res vinum, et tumultuosa ebrietas."

B 22b   M: Catella saginosa cecos catulos parit vel anus totus in yma descendit.
               [A fat bitch either gives birth to blind pups or her whole backside sinks down to
               the bottom.]

B 26a   S: Inter bonos et malos repletur domus.
               [Between good men and bad the house is filled.]
B 26b   M: Inter podiscos et merdam repletur latrina.
               [Between arse-wipes and shit the privy is filled.]

B 27a   S: Melius est habere dampnum in abscondito quam verecundiam in publico.
               [It is better to have one's loss in private than one's shame in public.]
B 27b   M: Bibere merdam desiderat qui canis culum basiat.
               [He desires to drink shit, who kisses a dog's ass.]

B 28a   S: Elemosinam desiderat facere qui alienum servum cupit ingeniosum esse.
               [He desires to perform a charity, who wishes another man's servant to be
               resourceful.]
B 28b   M: Qui furiosum castrat, merdam recentem bibere desiderat.
               [He that castrates a madman desires to drink fresh shit.]

B 29a   S: Hilarem datorem diligit Deus.[4]
               [God loves a cheerful giver.]
B 29b   M: Parum dat servienti qui cultellum suum lingit.
               [He gives too little to the server, who licks his own knife.]

B 30a   S: Duodecim manentes faciunt unam villam.
               [Twelve land-tenants make a village.]
B 30b   M: Duodecim torciones faciunt unam jussam.
               [Twelve cramps make a fart.]

B 31a   S: Duodecim vicarii faciunt unum comitatum.
               [Twelve viscounts make a county.]
B 31b   M: Duodecim bombi faciunt unum strontum.
               [Twelve loud farts make a turd.]

B 32a   S: Duodecim comites faciunt unum ducatum.
               [Twelve counts make a duchy.]
B 32b   M: Duodecim stronti faciunt unam paladam.
               [Twelve turds make a shovelful.]

B 33a   S: Duodecim duces faciunt unum regnum.
               [Twelve dukes make a kingdom.]
B 33b   M: Duodecim palade faciunt unam tinariam.
               [Twelve shovelfuls make a tubful.]

---

[4] 2 Corinthians 9:7: "hilarem enim datorem diligit Deus."

B 34a S: Duodecim regna faciunt unum imperium.
           [Twelve kingdoms make an empire.]
B 34b M: Duodecim tinarie faciunt unam carradam.
           [Twelve tubfuls make a cartful.]

B 36a S: Qui delicate nutrit servum ab infancia, postea senciet eum contumacem.[5]
           [He that nourishes his servant delicately from his childhood, afterwards shall
           find him stubborn.]
B 36b M: Nugax servus fetidos habet semper honores.
           [A worthless servant always holds honors foul.]

B 38a S: Quatuor evangeliste sustinent mundum.
           [The four evangelists uphold the world.]
B 38b M: Quatuor subposte sustinent latrinam, ne cadat qui sedet super eam.
           [Four posts uphold the privy, lest he fall in that sits over it.]

B 40a S: Optime convenit in clipeo candido nigra bucula.
           [A black boss fits perfectly on a white shield.]
B 40b M: Optime considet inter albas nates niger culus.
           [A black arsehole sits perfectly between white cheeks.]

B 42a S: Luna infra dies triginta peragit cursum suum.
           [The moon travels its course in thirty days.]
B 42b M: Culmus quantum ascendit in anno, tantum descendit in una die.
           [The stalk grows as much in a year, as it falls down in a single day.]

B 46a S: Eice derisorem et exibit cum eo jurgium cessabuntque cause et contumelie.[6]
           [Cast out the scoffer, and contention shall go out with him, and quarrels and
           reproaches shall cease.]
B 46b M: Eice inflacionem de ventre et exibit cum ea merda cessabuntque torciones et
           jusse.
           [Drive out wind from the belly, and shit shall go out with it, and cramps and
           farting shall cease.]

B 48a S: Inter duos montes unam vallem reperies.
           [Between two mountains you shall find a valley.]
B 48b M: Inter duo femora magna sepe latet vulva.
           [Between two large thighs often lies hidden a vulva.]

B 55a S: Cum homine litigioso non ineas pactum.
           [Make no covenant with the quarrelsome man.]

---

[5] Proverbs 29:21: "Qui delicate a pueritia nutrit servum suum postea sentiet eum contumacem."

[6] Proverbs 22:10: "Ejice derisorem, et exibit cum eo jurgium; cessabuntque causae et contumeliae."

B 55b   M: Vicioso incole si tres dantur uncie, non habet cor docile.
            [Even if a triple portion is given a wicked countryman, he won't have a gentle
            heart.]

B 60a   S: Venter meus dolet et fluctuat.
            [My belly is in pain and churning.]
B 60b   M: Vade ad latrinam, bene preme ventrem; culus evomat de quo fluctuat venter.
            [Go to the privy, press hard on your belly; your arse will get rid of what's
            making your belly churn.]

B 61a   S: Qui sibi nequam, cui bonus erit?
            [He that is evil to himself, to whom will he be good?][7]
B 61b   M: Cui placet hirnia, inhonestus debet esse.
            [The man that is pleased with his hernia must be depraved.]

B 62a   S: Si ascenderit super te spiritus potestatem habens, locum tuum ne dimiseris!
            [If the spirit of him that has power ascends upon you, leave not your place!][8]
B 62b   M: Quando hirnie gravescunt, testiculi marcescunt; cum venerit pluvia, fugit estus.
            [When a hernia gets heavy, the testicles decay; when the rains comes, the heat
            flees.]

B 66a   S: Si aliquando victoriam habueris super inimicum, cave ne incidas in manus
            illius!
            [If ever you should have victory over your enemy, beware lest you fall into his
            hands!][9]
B 66b   M: Qui in estate quiescit, in hyeme laborabit.
            [He who rests in summer, shall work in winter.]

B 69a   S: Qui timet pruinam, veniet super eum nix.
            [He that fears the hoary frost, the snow shall fall upon him.][10]
B 69b   M: Qui timet festucam numquam caccat in stipulam.
            [He that fears the stalk never shits in stubble.]

B 72a   S: Os mendax non habundat veritate.
            [A lying mouth does not abound in truth.][11]

---

[7] Ecclesiasticus 14:5: "Qui sibi nequam est, cui alii bonus erit."

[8] Ecclesiastes 10:4: "Si spiritus potestatem habentis ascenderit super te, locum tuum ne dimiseris."

[9] Compare Matthew 5:25: "Be at agreement with thy adversary betimes, whilst thou art in the way with him: lest perhaps the adversary deliver thee to the judge, and the judge deliver thee to the officer, and thou be cast into prison" ["Esto consentiens adversario tuo cito dum es in via cum eo; ne forte tradat te adversarius judici, et judex tradat te ministro, et in carcerem mittaris"].

[10] Compare Job 6:16: "They that fear the hoary frost, the snow shall fall upon them" ["Qui timent pruinam, irruet super eos nix"].

[11] Compare Proverbs 26:28: "A deceitful tongue loveth not truth" ["Lingua fallax non amat veritatem"].

B 72b   M: Expertus bucca de petulancia cui non prodest malum loquitur bonum.
              [A man skilled in impudent talk, when evil is unprofitable, speaks goodness.]

B 74a   S: Amicus et medicus in necessitate probantur.
              [A friend and a doctor are proven in time of need.][12]

B 74b   M: Adjuvat, non nocet, sepius bibit qui cellaria diligit.
              [He helps, he does no harm, he drinks more often, who likes a wine cellar.]

B 76a   S: Qui despicit parum, non meretur multum accipere.
              [He that scorns a little does not deserve to receive much.][13]

B 76b   M: Vulva despecta et canis incenatus tristes vadunt pausare.
              [A neglected vulva and an unfed dog go to bed sad.]

B 77a   S: Noli arguere derisorem, ne oderit te!
              [Rebuke not a scorner lest he hate you!][14]

B 77b   M: Quando aliquis plus movet merdam, plus fetet.
              [When somebody moves shit around more, it stinks more.]

B 78a   S: Non eligas cui bonum facias!
              [Do not choose for whom you would do good!][15]

B 78b   M: Perdit suas penas qui crasso porcello culum saginat.
              [He wastes his efforts who fattens the arse of a fat piglet.]

B 81a   S: Uxoris preces sobrias despicere noli.
              [A wife's sober prayers, do not scorn them.]

B 81b   M: Cum tua uxor vult sese uti, noli illi negare, quia necesse habet.
              [When your wife wants you to enjoy her, deny her not, since she has a need.]

B 88a   S: Considera que promittis, sed plenius quam promiseris presta.
              [Pay heed to what you promise, but give more generously than you promised.][16]

---

[12] Compare Ecclesiasticus 12:8-9: "A friend shall not be known in prosperity, and an enemy shall not be hidden in adversity. In the prosperity of a man, his enemies are grieved: and a friend is known in his adversity" ["Non agnoscetur in bonis amicus et non abscondetur in malis inimicus. In bonis viri inimici illius in tristitia et in malitia illius amicus agnitus est"].

[13] Proverbs 15:16: "Better is a little with the fear of the Lord, than great treasures without content" ["Melius est parum cum timore Domini, quam thesauri magni et insatiabiles"]; 16:8: "Better is a little with justice, than great revenues with iniquity" ["Melius est parum cum justitia quam multi fructus cum iniquitate"].

[14] Proverbs 9:8.

[15] The opposite view is presented at Ecclesiasticus 12:1: "If thou do good, know to whom thou dost it" ["Si benefeceris, scito cui feceris"].

[16] Compare Proverbs 25:14: "As clouds, and wind, when no rain followeth, so is the man that boasteth, and doth not fulfil his promises" ["Nubes et ventus, et pluviae non sequentes, vir gloriosus et promissa non complens"].

B 88b   M: In quantum habes longum saccum, tende pedem.
               [As long as the sack you have, stretch your foot that far.]

B 89a   S: Da sapienti occasionem, et addetur ei sapiencia.
               [Give a wise man an opportunity, and wisdom shall be added to him.][17]

B 89b   M: Infarcire ventrem et addetur tibi merda.
               [Stuff your belly, and shit shall be added to you.]

B 90a   S: Qui amat sapienciam, additur illi.
               [He that loves wisdom, more is added to him.]

B 90b   M: Laxa culum pedere, et ipse concuciet se.
               [Let the arsehole fart, and it will shake itself.]

B 91a   S: Bonum convivium malumque convivium suppis decoratum.
               [A good meal and a bad meal are enhanced by soups.]

B 91b   M: Suppe faciunt teneras buccas et culum viscosum.
               [Soups make the mouth tender and the arsehole sticky.]

B 98a   S: Melius est sedere in angulo solum quam cum muliere litigiosa.
               [It is better to sit in a corner all alone than with a quarrelsome woman.][18]

B 98b   M: Sorex que non potest ire ad suum foramen malleum ad suam caudam ligat.
               [The mouse that cannot go to its hole ties a hammer to its tail.]

B 107a   S: Sermo mollis frangit iram, sermo durus suscitat furorem.
               [Mild speech subdues anger, harsh speech rouses up fury.][19]

B 107b M: Irasci cui non potes nec finge te quasi noceas.
               [The man against whom you cannot show anger, do not pretend as if to harm him.]

B 108a   S: Cor mundum nichil timet.
               [A pure heart fears nothing.]

B 108b M: Qui sanum digitum ligat, sanum dissolvit.
               [He that binds up a healthy finger, unbinds a healthy one.]

B 109a   S: Cum tibi acciderit flagellum, noli murmurare sed gracias deo age et pacienter sustine.
               [If punishment should befall you, do not murmur, but give thanks to God and bear it patiently.]

B 109b M: Invitus basiat malamium cui in bucca nascitur dampnum.
               [Unwilling, he kisses cummin, in whose mouth an injury occurs.]

---

[17] Proverbs 9:9: "Give an occasion to a wise man, and wisdom shall be added to him."

[18] Compare Proverbs 21:9 and 25:24, "It is better to sit in a corner of the housetop, than with a brawling woman, and in a common house" ["Melius est sedere in angulo domatis, quam cum muliere litigiosa, et in domo communi"].

[19] Proverbs 15:1, reading *Responsio* for *Sermo*.

B 112a S: Ante os clybani non nascitur herba; et si nata fuerit, cito arescit a calore ignis.
             [Before the mouth of an oven, grass does not sprout, and if it should sprout, it
             quickly withers from the fire's heat.]
B 112b M: In culo non nascuntur pili; et si nati fuerint, cito uruntur propter aquas calidas,
             que per alvum de vicino discurrunt.
             [In an arsehole, hairs do not sprout; and if they should sprout, they are quickly
             scorched due to the hot waters coursing through the bowels nearby.]

B 114a S: Sicut malum inter ligna silvarum, sic amica mea inter filias.
             [As the apple tree among the trees of the woods, so is my beloved among
             daughters.][20]
B 114b M: Mel male habentibus ponitur.
             [Honey is set out for those feeling poorly.]

B 115a S: Circa aures stultus es et de fama plenus, reliqua parte corporis sordidus.
             [About your ears, you are a fool and full of gossip, vile in every other part of
             your body.]
B 115b M: Ubi invenis talem follem, bucca illum basia aut in culo morde.
             [When you find such a fool, kiss him on the mouth or bite him on the arse.]

B 121a S: Summo opere cave ne illi qui tibi carus amicus est des exiguum munus.
             [Take great care not to give a trifling gift to him who is your dear friend.]
B 121b M: Si amico tuo invitus das munera, perdis amicum tuum et munera.
             [If you give gifts to your friend unwillingly, you lose your friend and your gifts.]

B 125a S: Qui habet malam uxorem non potest securus esse.
             [He that has a bad wife cannot be free of cares.]
B 125b M: Qui habet caballum pravum non debet eum lassare ociosum.
             [He that has a bad horse must not leave him idle.]

B 128a S: Celum quando nubilat, pluviam facere vult.
             [When the sky clouds, it wants to rain.]
B 128b M: Canis quando crupitat, cacare vult.
             [When the dog hunches his back, he wants to shit.]

B 134a S: Beatus homo qui semper est pavidus.
             [Blessed is the man that is always fearful.][21]
B 134b M: Tarde clamat quem lupus strangulat.
             [He cries out too late whom a wolf is throttling.]

B 135a S: Suspiciosus homo numquam requiescit.
             [The suspicious man is never at peace.]

---

[20] Compare Canticle 2:3: "Sicut malus inter ligna silvarum, sic dilectus meus inter filios."

[21] Proverbs 28:14.

B 135b M: Cornarius duo patitur, dampnum et obprobrium.
           [The cuckold suffers two things, injury and vilification.]

B 138a S: Benefac justo et invenies retribucionem magnam; et si non ab ipso, certe a
           Domino.
           [Do good to the just, and you shall find great recompense; and if not of him,
           assuredly of the Lord.][22]

B 138b M: Benefac ventri et invenies eructuacionem magnam, et si non ab ore, certe a culo.
           [Do good to the belly, and you shall find great belching, and if not of the
           mouth, assuredly of the arsehole.]

---

[22] Ecclesiasticus 12:2.

❧ BIBLIOGRAPHY

Audelay, John the Blind. *The Poems of John Audelay*. Ed. Ella Keats Whiting. EETS o.s. 184. London: Oxford University Press, 1931.

———. *Poems and Carols (Oxford, Bodleian Library MS Douce 302)*. Ed. Susanna Fein. Kalamazoo, MI: Medieval Institute Publications, 2009.

Bakhtin, Mikhail. *Rabelais and His World*. Trans. Hélène Iswolsky. Cambridge: Massachusetts Institute of Technology, 1968. Rpt. Bloomington: Indiana University Press, 1984.

Beecher, Donald, ed. *The Dialogue of Solomon and Marcolphus*. Ottawa: Dovehouse Editions, 1995.

Ben-Amos, Dan, ed. *Folktales of the Jews*. 2 vols. Philadelphia: Jewish Publication Society, 2006–07.

Benary, Walter, ed. *Salomon et Marcolfus: Kritischer Text mit Einleitung, Anmerkungen, Übersicht über die Sprüche, Namen- und Wörterverzeichnis*. Heidelberg: C. Winter, 1914.

Blake, N. F. "William Caxton." In *Authors of the Middle Ages*. No. 7 in vol. 3: *English Writers of the Late Middle Ages*. Ed. M. C. Seymour. Aldershot: Ashgate Variorum, 1996. Pp. 1–68.

———, ed. *The History of Reynard the Fox Translated from the Dutch Original by William Caxton*. EETS o.s. 263. London: Oxford University Press, 1970.

———. *Caxton's Own Prose*. London: Andre Deutsch, 1973.

Blamires, Alcuin. "Women and Creative Intelligence in Medieval Thought." In *Voices in Dialogue: Reading Women in the Middle Ages*. Ed. Linda Olson and Kathryn Kerby-Fulton. Notre Dame, IN: University of Notre Dame Press, 2005. Pp. 213–30.

———, ed. *Woman Defamed and Woman Defended: An Anthology of Medieval Texts*. Oxford: Clarendon Press, 1992.

Bose, Mishtooni. "From Exegesis to Appropriation: The Medieval Solomon." *Medium Aevum* 65 (1996), 187–210.

Bouchard, Constance Brittain. *"Every Valley Shall Be Exalted": The Discourse of Opposites in Twelfth-Century Thought*. Ithaca, NY: Cornell University Press, 2003.

Bradbury, Nancy Mason. "Rival Wisdom in the Latin *Dialogue of Solomon and Marcolf*." *Speculum* 83 (2008), 331–65.

Braekman, Willy L., and Peter S. Macaulay. "The Story of the Cat and the Candle in Middle English Literature." *Neuphilologische Mitteilungen* 70 (1969), 690–702.

Brown, Catherine. *Contrary Things: Exegesis, Dialectic, and the Poetics of Didacticism*. Stanford, CA: Stanford University Press, 1998.

Camille, Michael. *Image on the Edge: The Margins of Medieval Art*. Cambridge, MA: Harvard University Press, 1992.

Chaucer, Geoffrey. *The Riverside Chaucer*. Third edition. Gen. ed. Larry D. Benson. Boston: Houghton Mifflin, 1987.

Cooper, Helen. "Sources and Analogues of Chaucer's *Canterbury Tales*: Reviewing the Work." *Studies in the Age of Chaucer* 19 (1997), 183–210.

Cortese-Pagani, Gina. "Il 'Bertoldo' di Guilio Cesare Croce ed i suoi fonti." *Studi Medievali* 3 (1911), 533–602.

Corti, Maria. "Models and Antimodels in Medieval Culture." Trans. John Meddemmen. *New Literary History* 10 (1979), 339–66.

Cosquin, Emmanuel. "Le Conte du chat et de la chandelle dans l'Europe du moyen âge et en Orient." *Romania* 40 (1911), 371–430 and 481–531.

Curschmann, Michael. "Marcolfus deutsch, mit einem Faksimile des Prosa-Drucks von M. Ayrer (1487)." In *Kleinere Erzählformen des 15. und 16. Jahrhunderts*. Ed. Walter Haug and Burghart Wachinger. Tübingen: Niemeyer, 1993. Pp. 151–255.

———. "Marcolf or Aesop? The Question of Identity in Visio-Verbal Contexts." *Studies in Iconography* 21 (2000), 1–45.

Davis, Natalie Zemon. "Proverbial Wisdom and Popular Errors." In *Society and Culture in Early Modern France: Eight Essays*. Stanford, CA: Stanford University Press, 1975. Pp. 227–67.

Du Cange, Charles Du Fresne, ed. *Glossarium Mediae et Infimae Latinitatis*. 7 vols. Paris: F. Didot, 1840–50.

Duff, E. Gordon, ed. *The Dialogue or Communing between the Wise King Salomon and Marcolphus*. London: Lawrence & Bullen, 1892.

Fein, Susanna, ed. *My Wyl and My Wrytyng: Essays on John the Blind Audelay*. Kalamazoo, MI: Medieval Institute Publications, 2009.

Freedman, Paul. *Images of the Medieval Peasant*. Stanford, CA: Stanford University Press, 1999.

Freidank. *Fridankes Bescheidenheit*. Ed. H. E. Bezzenberger. Halle: Waisenhaus, 1872.

Ginzberg, Louis. *The Legends of the Jews*. Trans. Henrietta Szold. 7 vols. Philadelphia: Jewish Publication Society of America, 1937–66.

Goddard, R. N. B. "Marcabru, *Li Proverbe au Vilain*, and the Tradition of Rustic Proverbs." *Neuphilologische Mitteilungen* 88 (1987), 55–70.

Gower, John. *Confessio Amantis*. In *The Complete Works of John Gower*. Ed. G. C. Macaulay. 4 vols. Oxford: Oxford University Press, 1899–1902. Vols. 2 and 3.

Gravdal, Kathryn. *Vilain and Courtois: Transgressive Parody in French Literature of the Twelfth and Thirteenth Centuries*. Lincoln: University of Nebraska Press, 1989.

Green, Richard Firth. "Marcolf the Fool and Blind John Audelay." In *Speaking Images: Essays in Honor of V. A. Kolve*. Ed. R. F. Yeager and Charlotte C. Morse. Asheville, NC: Pegasus Press, 2001. Pp. 559–76.

———. "Langland and Audelay." In *My Wyl and My Wrytyng: Essays on John the Blind Audelay*. Ed. Susanna Fein. Kalamazoo, MI: Medieval Institute Publications, 2009. Pp. 153–69.

Griese, Sabine. *Salomon und Markolf: ein literarischer Komplex im Mittelalter und in der frühen Neuzeit*. Tübingen: Niemeyer, 1999.

Hanning, Robert W. *The Individual in Twelfth-Century Romance*. New Haven: Yale University Press, 1977.

Hellinga, L. "*Dialogus creaturarum moralisatus*. Gouda: Gheraert Leeu, 31 August 1482." In *Vision of a Collector: The Lessing J. Rosenwald Collection in the Library of Congress*. Washington, DC: Library of Congress, 1991. Pp. 91–95.

Hellinga, Lotte, and J. B. Trapp, eds. *The Cambridge History of the Book in Britain*. Vol. 3: 1400–1557. Cambridge: Cambridge University Press, 1999.

Hellinga, Wytze Gs., with introductory essays by H. de la Fontaine Verwey, and G. W. Ovink. *Copy and Print in the Netherlands: An Atlas of Historical Bibliography*. Amsterdam: North-Holland Publishing Co., 1962.

Hellinga, Wytze Gs., and Lotte Hellinga. *The Fifteenth-Century Printing Types of the Low Countries*. 2 vols. Amsterdam: M. Hertzberger, 1966.

Henryson, Robert. *Poems*. Ed. Charles Elliott. Oxford: Clarendon Press, 1963.

Heywood, John. *Works and Miscellaneous Short Poems*. Ed. Burton A. Milligan. Urbana: University of Illinois Press, 1956.

Hirsch, Rudolf. *Printing, Selling and Reading 1450–1550*. Wiesbaden: Otto Harrassowitz, 1964.

Hunt, Tony. "Solomon and Marcolf." In *"Por le soie amisté": Essays in Honor of Norris J. Lacy*. Ed. Keith Busby and Catherine M. Jones. Amsterdam: Rodopi, 2000. Pp. 199–224.

Jones, Malcolm. "Marcolf the Trickster in Late Mediaeval Art and Literature or: The Mystery of the Bum in the Oven." In *Spoken in Jest.* Ed. Gillian Bennett. Sheffield: Sheffield Academic Press, 1991. Pp. 139–74.

Kay, Sarah. *Courtly Contradictions: The Emergence of the Literary Object in the Twelfth Century.* Stanford, CA: Stanford University Press, 2001.

Kemble, John M. *The Dialogue of Salomon and Saturnus with an Historical Introduction.* London: Ælfric Society, 1848.

Kurath, Hans, and Sherman M. Kuhn. *Middle English Dictionary.* Ann Arbor: University of Michigan Press, 1952.

Kuskin, William. *Symbolic Caxton: Literary Culture and Print Capitalism.* Notre Dame, IN: University of Notre Dame Press, 2008.

———, ed. *Caxton's Trace: Studies in the History of English Printing.* Notre Dame, IN: University of Notre Dame Press, 2006.

Lambert of Ardres. *Historia Comitum Ghisnensium.* Ed. Johannes Heller. Monumenta Germaniae Historica 24. Hanover: Hahn, 1879. Pp. 550–642.

———. *The History of the Counts of Guines and Lords of Ardres.* Trans. Leah Shopkow. Philadelphia: University of Pennsylvania Press, 2001.

Langland, William. *The Vision of Piers Plowman: A Complete Edition of the B-Text.* Ed. A. V. C. Schmidt. London: J. M. Dent, 1978.

Latham, R. E., ed. *Revised Medieval Latin Word-List: From British and Irish Sources.* London: Oxford University Press, 1965.

Latham, R. E., and D. R. Howlett. *Dictionary of Medieval Latin from British Sources.* 12 vols. to date. London: Oxford University Press, 1975–.

Lewis, Cameron. "Proverbs, Precepts, and Monitory Pieces." In *A Manual of the Writings in Middle English, 1050–1500.* Ed. J. Burke Severs, Albert E. Hartung, and Peter G. Beidler. 11 vols. to date. New Haven: Connecticut Academy of Arts and Sciences, 1967–. 9:2957–3048, 3349–3404.

Li Proverbe Au Vilain: A Critical Edition. Ed. John Bednar. New Orleans: University Press of the South, 2000.

Lydgate, John. *The Minor Poems of John Lydgate: Edited from All Available Manuscripts, with an Attempt to Establish the Lydgate Canon. Vol. 2: Secular Poems.* Ed. Henry Noble MacCracken. EETS o.s. 192. London: Oxford University Press, 1934.

Marini, Quinto. "La dissacrazione come strumento di affermazione ideologica. Una lettura del 'Dialogo di Salomone e Marcolfo.'" *Studi Medievali,* third series 28 (1987), 667–705.

———, ed. *Il dialogo di Salomone e Marcolfo.* Rome: Salerno, 1991.

Menner, Robert J., ed. *The Poetical Dialogues of Solomon and Saturn.* London: Oxford University Press, 1941.

O'Brien O'Keeffe, Katherine. "The Geographic List of *Solomon and Saturn II.*" *Anglo-Saxon England* 20 (1991), 123–41.

Orme, Nicholas. *Education and Society in Medieval and Renaissance England.* London: Hambledon Press, 1989.

Pearsall, Derek. "Audelay's *Marcolf and Solomon* and the Langlandian Tradition." In *My Wyl and My Wrytyng: Essays on John the Blind Audelay.* Ed. Susanna Fein. Kalamazoo, MI: Medieval Institute Publications, 2009. Pp. 138–52.

Raimbaut d'Orange. *The Life and Works of the Troubadour Raimbaut d'Orange.* Ed. Walter T. Pattison. Minneapolis: University of Minnesota Press, 1952.

Scattergood, V. J. "'The Debate between Nurture and Kynd' — An Unpublished Middle English Poem." *Notes and Queries* 215 (1970): 244–46.

Schorbach, Karl. "Eine Buchanzeige des Antwerpener Druckers Geraert Leeu in niederländischer Sprache (1491)." *Zeitschrift für Bücherfreunde* 9, no. 4 (1905/06), 139–48.

Simpson, James. "Saving Satire after Arundel's *Constitutions*: John Audelay's 'Marcol and Solomon.'" In *Text and Controversy from Wyclif to Bale: Essays in Honour of Anne Hudson.* Ed. Helen Barr and Ann M. Hutchison. Turnhout: Brepols, 2005. Pp. 387–404.

Singer, Samuel. *Sprichwörter des Mittelalters.* 3 vols. Bern: Herbert Lang & CIE, 1944–47.

Solterer, Helen. *The Master and Minerva: Disputing Women in French Medieval Culture.* Berkeley: University of California Press, 1995.

Steiner, Arpad. "The Vernacular Proverb in Mediaeval Latin Prose." *American Journal of Philology* 65 (1944), 37–68.

Stump, Eleonore. *Dialectic and Its Place in the Development of Medieval Logic.* Ithaca, NY: Cornell University Press, 1989.

Utley, Francis Lee. "Dialogues, Debates, and Catechisms." In *A Manual of the Writings in Middle English, 1050–1500.* Ed. J. Burke Severs, Albert E. Hartung, and Peter G. Beidler. 11 vols. to date. New Haven: Connecticut Academy of Arts and Sciences, 1967–. 3:669–745, 829–902.

Vreese, Willem de, and Jan de Vries, eds. *Dat dyalogus of twisprake tusschen den wisen coninck Salomon ende Marcolphus.* Leiden: E. J. Brill, 1941.

Welsford, Enid. *The Fool: His Social and Literary History.* London: Faber and Faber, 1935.

Whiting, Bartlett Jere, with the collaboration of Helen Wescott Whiting. *Proverbs, Sentences, and Proverbial Phrases from English Writings Mainly before 1500.* Cambridge, MA: The Belknap Press of Harvard University Press, 1968.

William of Tyre. *Chronicon.* Ed. R. B. C. Huygens, H. E. Mayer, and Gerhard Rösch. 2 vols. Corpus Christianorum Continuatio Mediaevalis 63–63A. Turnholt: Brepols, 1986.

Ziolkowski, Jan M. "The Deeds of Aesop and Marcolf." In *Scripturus vitam : lateinische Biographie von der Antike bis in die Gegenwart: Festgabe für Walter Berschin zum 65. Geburtstag.* Ed. Dorothea Walz. Heidelberg: Mattes, 2002. Pp. 105–23.

———. *Solomon and Marcolf.* Harvard Studies in Medieval Latin 1. Cambridge, MA: Harvard University Press, 2008.

✒ MIDDLE ENGLISH TEXTS SERIES

Stanzaic Guy of Warwick, edited by Alison Wiggins (2004)

Saints' Lives in Middle English Collections, edited by E. Gordon Whatley, with Anne B. Thompson and Robert K. Upchurch (2004)

Siege of Jerusalem, edited by Michael Livingston (2004)

The Kingis Quair and Other Prison Poems, edited by Linne R. Mooney and Mary-Jo Arn (2005)

The Chaucerian Apocrypha: A Selection, edited by Kathleen Forni (2005)

John Gower, *The Minor Latin Works*, edited and translated by R. F. Yeager, with *In Praise of Peace*, edited by Michael Livingston (2005)

Sentimental and Humorous Romances: Floris and Blancheflour, Sir Degrevant, The Squire of Low Degree, The Tournament of Tottenham, and The Feast of Tottenham, edited by Erik Kooper (2006)

The Dicts and Sayings of the Philosophers, edited by John William Sutton (2006)

Everyman and Its Dutch Original, Elckerlijc, edited by Clifford Davidson, Martin W. Walsh, and Ton J. Broos (2007)

The N-Town Plays, edited by Douglas Sugano, with assistance by Victor I. Scherb (2007)

The Book of John Mandeville, edited by Tamarah Kohanski and C. David Benson (2007)

John Lydgate, *The Temple of Glas*, edited by J. Allan Mitchell (2007)

The Northern Homily Cycle, edited by Anne B. Thompson (2008)

Codex Ashmole 61: A Compilation of Popular Middle English Verse, edited by George Shuffelton (2008)

Chaucer and the Poems of "Ch," edited by James I. Wimsatt (revised edition 2009)

William Caxton, *The Game and Playe of the Chesse*, edited by Jenny Adams (2009)

John the Blind Audelay, *Poems and Carols*, edited by Susanna Fein (2009)

Two Moral Interludes: The Pride of Life and Wisdom, edited by David Klausner (2009)

John Lydgate, *Mummings and Entertainments*, edited by Claire Sponsler (2010)

Mankind, edited by Kathleen M. Ashley and Gerard NeCastro (2010)

The Castle of Perseverance, edited by David N. Klausner (2010)

Robert Henryson, *The Complete Works*, edited by David J. Parkinson (2010)

John Gower, *The French Balades*, edited and translated by R. F. Yeager (2011)

The Middle English Metrical Paraphrase of the Old Testament, edited by Michael Livingston (2011)

The York Corpus Christi Plays, edited by Clifford Davidson (2011)

Prik of Conscience, edited by James H. Morey (2012)

🖉 COMMENTARY SERIES

Haimo of Auxerre, *Commentary on the Book of Jonah*, translated with an introduction and notes by Deborah Everhart (1993)

Medieval Exegesis in Translation: Commentaries on the Book of Ruth, translated with an introduction and notes by Lesley Smith (1996)

Nicholas of Lyra's Apocalypse Commentary, translated with an introduction and notes by Philip D. W. Krey (1997)

Rabbi Ezra Ben Solomon of Gerona, *Commentary on the Song of Songs and Other Kabbalistic Commentaries*, selected, translated, and annotated by Seth Brody (1999)

John Wyclif, *On the Truth of Holy Scripture*, translated with an introduction and notes by Ian Christopher Levy (2001)

Second Thessalonians: Two Early Medieval Apocalyptic Commentaries, introduced and translated by Steven R. Cartwright and Kevin L. Hughes (2001)

The "Glossa Ordinaria" on the Song of Songs, translated with an introduction and notes by Mary Dove (2004)

The Seven Seals of the Apocalypse: Medieval Texts in Translation, translated with an introduction and notes by Francis X. Gumerlock (2009)

The "Glossa Ordinaria" on Romans, translated with an introduction and notes by Michael Scott Woodward (2011)

🐝 Documents of Practice Series

Love and Marriage in Late Medieval London, selected, translated, and introduced by Shannon McSheffrey (1995)

Sources for the History of Medicine in Late Medieval England, selected, introduced, and translated by Carole Rawcliffe (1995)

A Slice of Life: Selected Documents of Medieval English Peasant Experience, edited, translated, and with an introduction by Edwin Brezette DeWindt (1996)

Regular Life: Monastic, Canonical, and Mendicant "Rules," selected and introduced by Douglas J. McMillan and Kathryn Smith Fladenmuller (1997); second edition, selected and introduced by Daniel Marcel La Corte and Douglas J. McMillan (2004)

Women and Monasticism in Medieval Europe: Sisters and Patrons of the Cistercian Reform, selected, translated, and with an introduction by Constance H. Berman (2002)

Medieval Notaries and Their Acts: The 1327–1328 Register of Jean Holanie, introduced, edited, and translated by Kathryn L. Reyerson and Debra A. Salata (2004)

John Stone's Chronicle: Christ Church Priory, Canterbury, 1417–1472, selected, translated, and introduced by Meriel Connor (2010)

🐝 Medieval German Texts in Bilingual Editions Series

Sovereignty and Salvation in the Vernacular, 1050–1150, introduction, translations, and notes by James A. Schultz (2000)

Ava's New Testament Narratives: "When the Old Law Passed Away," introduction, translation, and notes by James A. Rushing, Jr. (2003)

History as Literature: German World Chronicles of the Thirteenth Century in Verse, introduction, translation, and notes by R. Graeme Dunphy (2003)

Thomasin von Zirclaria, *Der Welsche Gast (The Italian Guest)*, translated by Marion Gibbs and Winder McConnell (2009)

Ladies, Whores, and Holy Women: A Sourcebook in Courtly, Religious, and Urban Cultures of Late Medieval Germany, introductions, translations, and notes by Ann Marie Rasmussen and Sarah Westphal-Wihl (2010)

🐝 Varia

The Study of Chivalry: Resources and Approaches, edited by Howell Chickering and Thomas H. Seiler (1988)

Studies in the Harley Manuscript: The Scribes, Contents, and Social Contexts of British Library MS Harley 2253, edited by Susanna Fein (2000)

The Liturgy of the Medieval Church, edited by Thomas J. Heffernan and E. Ann Matter (2001; second edition 2005)

Johannes de Grocheio, *Ars musice*, edited and translated by Constant J. Mews, John N. Crossley, Catherine Jeffreys, Leigh McKinnon, and Carol J. Williams (2011)

🐝 To Order Please Contact:

Medieval Institute Publications
Western Michigan University
Kalamazoo, MI 49008-5432
Phone (269) 387-8755
FAX (269) 387-8750
http://www.wmich.edu/medieval/mip/index.html

Typeset in 10/13 New Baskerville
and Golden Cockerel Ornaments display
Designed by Linda K. Judy
Manufactured by Cushing-Malloy, Inc.

Medieval Institute Publications
College of Arts and Sciences
Western Michigan University
1903 W. Michigan Avenue
Kalamazoo, MI 49008-5432
http://www.wmich.edu/medieval/mip

 WESTERN MICHIGAN UNIVERSITY